A Blueprint for Hope

Raise Your Autistic Child Alongside Jesus

Gina Badalaty

May the God of hope fill you with all joy and peace in believing, so that
by the power of the Holy Spirit you may abound in hope.
— Romans 15:13, ESV

Bright
COMMUNICATIONS

CONTENTS

Introduction

Parenting is a difficult and challenging job, full of unexpected issues that you cannot possibly predict.

But when your child is diagnosed with autism, that job becomes a great deal more challenging — and it can be frightening as well.

It doesn't have to be that way. I'm Gina Badalaty, and I'm the mother of two children with special needs. My husband, Chris, and I have an older daughter with Down syndrome, Amelia, and a younger daughter, Zoe, with severe autism. They both face different challenges, some that they've overcome and others that seem more permanent.

Amelia was an easy baby and is often a calming presence in our family. But like many autistic children, Zoe had great difficulty from early on. She struggled to communicate her needs and her discomfort, an issue that Amelia never had. While parenting any child with a disability has its obstacles, it's much more confusing when your child cannot share his or her needs.

Initially, Zoe cried so much as a baby that we simply assumed she was fussy. But with time, we learned that she had sensory issues which were causing her problems.

By the time she was two years old, we knew something was wrong. Zoe hadn't slept for more than a few hours in a row her entire life – and this pattern continued through age five. She banged her head when she was frustrated, had frequent meltdowns, and was more likely to mouth toys than play with them properly. The early development team came to our home and diagnosed her with sensory processing disorder. I was not yet educated enough about the topic to understand it. I thought it was a minor issue that would be resolved through therapy. Surely, in a few months, things would change.

At age three, it became apparent that Zoe had significant speech delays, even though she knew the alphabet backwards and forwards. This time, we took her to a developmental pediatrician, who diagnosed her with autism.

("Or PDD-NOS, if you prefer.") I was heartbroken. I thought the sensory issues were temporary and fixable.

I also believed that autism was a devastating diagnosis, to be feared.

Thanks to fear and stress, those first few years were a challenge. Zoe went through phases that were not only difficult but also harmful. Autism comes with a host of challenges that can put your child at serious risk. Over the years, we learned unique strategies, uncommon approaches, and ideas that had the so-called "experts" scratching their heads about how they led to Zoe being a calmer, happier, and safer child. This allowed our daughter the space to develop her personality and shine in the ways that God meant for her to shine.

We've also learned that finding an approach that can help her with some of her challenges is not a one-time adjustment. Puberty threw many of her gains out the window. And years later, there are many challenges she still may not overcome.

This is a hard truth that may be the reality for your child his or her entire life.

But you are not alone. Jesus is right there, walking beside you.

This path is not easy, but the Lord knows this. As Zoe got older, she faced more obstacles. And again, some of these we overcame. Other things we expected would go away did not. It's likely that Zoe will always need some type of care.

But I know that God created her with a purpose because when Amelia was little, I had a vision of another dark-haired baby girl in the car seat before Zoe was even created.

Zoe has taught us so much, like how to fight for the people you love, how to love someone through a difficult time, and how to value and honor a person even when they can't express themselves. In this way, she saved us as we strove to help her.

And that's how we should treat her: like a little bit of salvation for our family. For even God's salvation came with pain and sacrifice; so why not the little girl who led us on a path that changed our lives so we can change others?

Those challenges help us adults understand what's really important. Do I really believe I'd be this close to God without her? Hasn't she caused me to look further, pray deeper, and trust harder in my Jesus? Wouldn't my faith still be surface level? Would I have fought as hard for my marriage? Would I know anything about clean living and the power of health, detox, the mind, or the long-suffering love of the Father?

I doubt it. This is all for this little girl of mine. And I am grateful with all my heart that this angel came into our home.

So, take a deep breath. In the pages ahead, we'll dig into the techniques that will help you stay calm and levelheaded—for the most part. You'll learn to let the Lord help your child blossom into the fearfully and wonderfully made person he or she was designed to be.

Chapter 1

Finding the Peace of Christ
on This Journey

I am leaving you with a gift — peace of mind and heart. And the peace I give is a gift the world cannot give. So don't be troubled or afraid. — John 14:27, NLT

I know how it feels. There is no such thing as a "typical" day anymore.

Or rather, what has become a typical day is nothing like you imagined when you were carrying your precious child in your womb.

Perhaps you spent the morning preventing your toddler from bashing his head against the wall or defending yourself from your child's skin-breaking bites. Maybe you walked in the bedroom to find your child eating a light bulb. Maybe the day started out fine, but you can't get your child on the school bus and you don't know why. Or you've ended your evening cleaning marker off walls, food off the ceiling, and feces off the floor.

It hurts because you know there is a beautiful, precious person inside this raging storm. You've seen the glimpses of tenderness, the flashes of brilliance, and the hints of joy.

You just don't see it enough. Your senses are overwhelmed by an onslaught of sounds and smells no one ever told you that you would have to deal with raising a child.

What you do see is a child in pain who cannot be helped. You've tried hard to be positive, you've sought support and respite, and you've applied for waivers and resources. You've bought every book on the subject and spent hours doing online research, and yet you still find yourself in so much mental pain you can barely breathe.

When you should be sound asleep, you seek respite by being locked deeply into a novel, social media or TV, needing some type of escape from the day before you can face another.

There is a better way.

Nothing but the Blood of Jesus

Right now, you feel lost. Your burdens are too hard. You can't understand how you'll make it through another day. Worse yet, you see other moms who are skating through life, complaining that their child didn't make some team or failed a test, while you worry if your child will ever hold a job or have a friend.

No one gets it. No one gets you. And no one cares about your child.

But that's not true. There is One who cares about every single hair on your child's head and yours too. Jesus sees and knows all you are going through. He is behind the scenes, waiting for you to turn to Him.

The Son of God pulled Himself out of His heavenly throne to be born on this Earth to a poor Jewish girl named Mary. She had very little but her faith, but that was all she needed in order to be blessed among women by carrying and birthing the baby Jesus, her own Lord and Savior.

After He grew up and started His ministry, He remained poor. He had "no place to lay His head" (Luke 9:58), but what He did have was enough: His Father and the Word.

And those blessings can be enough for you too.

During His time on Earth, our Lord walked miles around the ancient world to serve the people in towns both near and far from His birthplace. He healed the sick, He cast out demons, and He even raised the dead. He performed so many miracles that the last sentence of the gospel of John says, "Jesus did many other things as well. If every one of them were written down, I suppose that even the whole world would not have room for the books that would be written." (John 21:25, NIV)

When He completed this ministry of service, He then did His greatest work: He laid down His life to pay off our sins. He made that sacrifice for you and me and everyone who is need of a savior, which is all of us. He willingly allowed His enemies to torture, mock, and nail Him to the cross that He carried Himself. Then He gave up His spirit and died, all for our salvation.

It's a bitter thing to remember and read about in the scriptures, but God the Father needed Jesus' sacrifice so you don't have to pay the price for all your sins. He's got it covered.

Think about that: Every single sin you've ever done, big or small, is wiped away the moment you accept Jesus' sacrifice on your behalf. And in that moment, you become an adopted child of God, a greatly treasured child, and an heir to His kingdom. You have the privilege and the right to be able to speak to God Himself, asking Him for your needs directly, secure in the knowledge that right now, He is preparing a place for you in eternity.

No one can ever take that away. *No one.*

Maybe you don't know yet who Jesus is but you felt drawn to purchase this book. If that's you, I invite you to read along and reach out to me via my website or email with questions. If you're curious about the Bible, a good place to start is the gospel of John. Just read it through, and I will pray that God reveals Himself to you.

Maybe you have sought Jesus for comfort. You haven't accepted Him as your Savior yet. You are not quite there yet but you are intrigued by the love you see in your Christian friends and family. I pray that through this book, you will discover Christ's love for you and fall deeply in love with Him too.

Maybe you do understand that Jesus is your Lord and Savior, and you've come to Him, but it doesn't feel like enough. I get that too. We need to walk this life day by day, with an enemy who is constantly trying to turn us away from God. Satan will use every opportunity to distract you with your child's challenges and use them to hurt you or worse, pull you away from the Lord. I pray you can use this book to further turn your heart to the Lord, even when you fail, struggle, or feel like giving up.

No matter where you are in your walk with Jesus, only He can provide the kind of peace parents like us need.

Right now, the peace you are seeking may not be the right kind. As Jesus says in John 14:27, His peace is not the peace of the world. It's not the "kick back and enjoy a warm bath" kind. It's not comfort and luxury, rest and relaxation, a night out with the girls, pride in our kids' accomplishments, or success in their grades. It's not a "cushion" in our bank account, a child with a bright future, or friendships with popular people.

Our lives more frequently look like the very opposite of that: struggles with family, marital difficulties, living paycheck to paycheck, and a completely uncertain future for your child, both now and once you are gone.

What is Jesus' peace? It's the knowledge that God is there for you. He always has your back—always! God is in full control, and nothing that happens to you or your child is a surprise to Him. If you are a follower of Christ, Jesus promises this:

> And we know that all things work together for good to those who love God, to those who are the called according to His purpose. — Romans 8:28

This is true even when things seem impossible. He allows trials and tribulations partly so that we are molded into the people He created us to be.

But He also allows these trials to teach us that only in our weakness can He be strong. We need to let the Lord do the heavy lifting in our parenting.

And boy, is that hard! As moms, we want to fix everything for our children. We take our kids' setbacks personally.

But Jesus only gets the glory when you let Him do the work. And will that change you? It certainly will. How? You'll be a better parent. A better witness. A better Christian.

If God's ultimate purpose for His children is to spread the Good News, what better person to help other parents suffering and struggling to raise a child on the autism spectrum than someone who's been through it all and has not lost hope?

First, though, we must attain this peace. How do we get there with so much pain and conflict in our minds?

Moving Forward with God's Help

In 1 Thessalonians 5:17, Paul gave the church instructions on how to live, and one of those directives was to "pray continually." A long time ago, I used to think this verse was a bit silly. Continually? Always? You must be joking! There's too much to do to pray continually. I have commitments, responsibilities, duties — and a child with severe autism.

One day, I was feeling exhausted and overwhelmed. I was on the brink of despair and just wanted to curl up into a ball and die. I was depressed and felt totally defeated.

I had been struggling with a lot, including financial difficulties, marital strain, and family problems. Some of my challenges at the time were due to certain struggles we were experiencing with Zoe. I was also struggling with my prayer life. I just didn't feel like I had the energy or desire to pray. I'd rather do something mindless, indulging in a book, TV, or games.

Then I realized that I was actually making things more difficult by not turning to the Lord. By avoiding Him, I started losing my faith in His reliability. My trust in Him was wavering. I had witnessed it in others many times, but suddenly I was gripped with fear and disbelief. I let the thought that God could not and would not do what I needed estrange me from Him.

As time went on, I became afraid to ask for what I wanted. Is praying for your child to become healed selfish? My daughter wasn't better and, in fact, had regressed. I'd somehow convinced myself that her healing was out of God's will so I just stopped asking.

Later that week, we had a Sunday service on prayer, and I was convicted when the pastor quoted James 4:2: "Yet you do not have because you do not ask."

It was as if the sermon had been written just for me.

After that, I started praying more boldly for my children. Soon, I started praying that way for my husband and myself, and I saw mountains move in unbelievable ways.

Not every obstacle was overcome, but I learned that God heals in His perfect timing.

And I noticed that the more I prayed, it seemed, the more I *could* pray.

Long ago, there was a *Saturday Night Live* skit where Phil Hartman played Jesus. He came to visit Sally Field, who asked him to help her not burn the rice. This Jesus told her he had bigger things to attend to, but Sally wouldn't listen. It's a funny skit that we discussed several years back in my small church. I thought this was common sense: It's silly to pray about your dinner not burning!

But a friend said, "But why *not* ask Him not to burn the rice, along with everything else?"

That really gave me pause. What if I started asking Him for help with the cooking? The ironic thing is cooking continues to be a difficult yet critical area for me to tend to for my children.

I should pray for help in the kitchen! Isn't it just another matter of trust? If I pray for help cooking, won't He be pleased that I am so reliant on Him? That I trust Him with small matters as well as big?

Trust in small things can lead to big things, and trust in big things can lead to amazing moments of joy, grace, and hope.

But even when you feel lifted up, our enemy is relentless. You can feel on fire with God, riding a wave of trust one day, and defeated by despair the next. You may even want to throw in the towel on parenting.

When You Want to Quit

When you're raising a child with disruptive challenges, the temptation of giving up can come into your mind. I know a lot about quitting because it's happened to me.

Oh, I still followed God. Gave Him the glory, praised Him, prayed, shared my heart.

But in reality, I had given up on my child. She was doing well, then puberty hit, and then she *wasn't*. And the easier solutions, the ones that seemed to work for every parent around me, did not.

And if all that weren't enough, my marriage hit a real crisis. Shortly after failed attempts to fix that problem, Covid-19 hit.

My daughter was not better. My husband and I separated. Discipline fell by the wayside as the ability to do activities dried up. My daughter refused to do remote school and then she was supposed to start high school, in a huge building she'd never entered, but there was no opportunity for transition. All of this was capped by an unexpected medical issue.

2020 became a year of putting out fires. There was no opportunity for forward motion because we were in flat-out survival mode, 24/7, for months and months.

As for me, I just gave up. What was the point? Bit by bit over the past five years, I had been giving up hope.

I was depressed and absent in spirit. I dug into distraction. I still talked to God daily, asking, praying, and begging, but little by little my prayer life was also distracted by these all-important activities of reading fiction and playing games on my phone. I had lost all hope.

Physically, I wasn't doing well either. I wasn't sick, but I had been experiencing fatigue, stress-induced hot flashes, and an odd stomach flutter and disconnectedness when I went to bed. Other parts of my health started to suffer. The activities that once helped me manage my stress seemed to have no improvement.

One day, I went to an event held by a chiropractor. He discussed the impact of stress and its connection to trauma. He laid out the unusual symptoms I'd been feeling that I could not explain. They were all related to post-traumatic stress disorder. I had PTSD! This explained so much that I breathed a sigh of relief at finally understanding what was wrong with me. We cannot live in crisis mode for a long time. Unchecked, long-term stress not only harms your body. It can throw your mental health for a loop.

Discovering this was not easy, but it was necessary to facilitate a true path to healing. And I needed that for myself before I could properly help my family.

And this is where calling on Jesus regularly has helped me. While dealing with these issues, I cannot neglect my kids' needs. To remain a strong mother to my children, I've organized my day to ensure I'm providing small things for them every single day: healthier meals, proper nutrients, regular bible reading, and telling them that they are loved — by me and by God.

I'm also making sure that I treat them with love and respect, even when my sinful nature wants to yell at them for things that are not their fault. I call on God in moments of extreme stress, which goes a long way to helping me calm down.

Jesus is enough for all our problems — big and small. So go ahead, ask Him to help you not burn the rice — or to get through something even small on a regular basis for your family — and ask Him for everything else too.

If we can pray for those things, we can learn to turn to Him as soon as ugly feelings crop up. Think about how your life would change if you turned your mind toward Jesus for help whenever these thoughts cropped up:

- Fear over your child's future
- Anger over how he or she was treated at school
- Anxiety about how you'll pay for his or her new treatment or protocol
- Envy when a friend's child is achieving great things
- Disappointment when plans are derailed by meltdowns
- Stress over losing income or services
- Feeling overwhelmed when things go wrong

Friends, if you have a child on the autism spectrum, praying continually should be your daily method of operation. Whenever you hear negative thoughts, doubts, fears, or worries in your brain, call out to Jesus. In His Name, pray for help to take "every thought captive to make it obedient to Christ" (2 Cor. 10:5 NIV). Ask this over and over, if you have to. God doesn't mind! In fact, He wants us to keep asking for all the things we need and want, as frequently as we can until He answers us.

Need proof? In Luke 11:5-12 (NIV) Jesus tells the parable of the persistent friend.

Then Jesus said to them, "Suppose you have a friend, and you go to him at midnight and say, 'Friend, lend me three loaves of bread; a friend of mine on a journey has come to me, and I have no food to offer him.' And suppose the one inside answers, 'Don't bother me. The door is already locked, and my children and I are in bed. I can't get up and give you anything.' I tell you, even though he will not get up and give you the bread because of friendship, yet because of your shameless audacity he will surely get up and give you as much as you need.

"So I say to you: Ask and it will be given to you; seek and you will find; knock and the door will be opened to you. For everyone who asks receives; the one who seeks finds; and to the one who knocks, the door will be opened.

"Which of you fathers, if your son asks for a fish, will give him a snake instead? Or if he asks for an egg, will give him a scorpion? If you then, though you are evil, know how to give good gifts to your children, how much more will your Father in heaven give the Holy Spirit to those who ask him!"

This story always gives me goosebumps! Do we really think our Father in Heaven will give us a snake or a scorpion? Of course not!

He is our true and perfect Father, and He will treat us as such. He longs to ease our pain and does — when He can. He will also allow us to suffer when it is best for our growth and His glory.

I experienced this type of grace firsthand. Before Zoe was born when Amelia was a baby, my mother was diagnosed with Alzheimer's disease. At the time, I could think of no worse fate. I was scared. I couldn't bear the agony that day. I turned again and again to God, asking Him to help me. My heartbreak was complete as the more I saw how much I'd lost her.

In those moments, I felt the comforting Hand of the Holy Spirit. It was an entire day of His divine comfort, as the painful thought of my mother's future returned to me over and over.

Each and every time I turned to the Lord, I felt a calmness and peace. By the end of the night, I was able to cope with the news. The Holy Spirit had taught me a valuable lesson about how faithful the Lord is when we turn to Him, no matter how often we ask for the same thing.

Turn your painful and discouraging thoughts over to the Lord, every day, every hour, every minute! Ask Him for the comfort you need to guide you as you raise your child. You never have to stop asking for His help. He is always there, ready to come to the aid of His children.

Coping with a New Autism Diagnosis

Years later, my daughter's autism diagnosis was as painful as my mother's Alzheimer's diagnosis. I remember it clearly because I cried on the drive home, and the teardrops clouded my ability to see what was in front of me.

Before that day, I had hoped that her sensory issues were a temporary problem easily fixed. I thought, *She doesn't have autism. She just has a few behaviors that therapy would soon resolve.* In my heart, I knew the truth, but it was easier to lie to myself since I didn't yet have an official diagnosis. Once I did know, I fed my doubt and the stigma by asking that she be labeled "PDD-NOS" rather than getting on official autism diagnosis.

Denying the truth, however, never helped me. What *did* help was moving forward with this new knowledge by putting my trust in Jesus. The following steps can help you cope with your child's diagnosis.

Acknowledge Your Pain

Here's the thing: This diagnosis hurts. As a Christian, you may feel that's not right. You could be tempted to hide your true emotions from God and yourself even when you know that's how you feel. The thing is, God already knows everything you're thinking and feeling. And He wants you to be totally honest with Him. But if you won't share it with Him, He will not press you on it.

God gave us free will, and part of that is respecting the choices you make in your relationship with Him. That's what following Jesus is—building a *relationship*. God is your Father, and your Lord, but He's also your friend, your teacher, and your parenting partner (along with your child's father, of course).

It's important to tell Him about your pain, disappointment, anger, and all your negative thoughts and responses. If you struggle with feeling guilty over being honest with the Lord, remember that He already knows what's in your heart. He wants to hear it from your lips!

When you cry out to Jesus with all you emotions, you are providing a way to work through the pain so that you can do what you need to do. Allow yourself to work through your feelings, no matter how often they crop up. When a new crisis arises related to my daughter's autism, I have to let it out.

Sometimes, I get frustrated because I think, *Shouldn't I be over this already?* But our parenting journey can have twists and turns we did not expect. Don't box yourself into being "the strong mom" all the time. Take the time to process your emotions without judgment by giving them to the Lord.

When Jesus shouldered that cross and walked all the way up the hill to Calvary where He was crucified, He did it once and for all to nail your sins to that Cross and relieve you of your eternal debt. He can do the same for all your burdens, from your grief and pain to all your ugly feelings about raising an autistic child, to the exhaustion you have when you serve anyone else you love.

If you don't give Him that burden, you can get stuck in the pain—and that's not going to help your child. Jesus gives you the strength to move forward so you can care for your child in the best way possible.

Accept Changes and Challenges

Autism is a rollercoaster ride. Change happens, and it's not always good. One day your child bangs his head. So you treat that behavior until it's gone, but now he won't wear a certain kind of clothing. At some point you master the clothing issue, and suddenly your potty-trained child will not sit on the toilet. It's a constant give and take, and sometimes it's one step forward, two or three back. And as your child grows up, you may find a whole new set of challenges to overcome.

There will be times that you find yourself scratching your head, wondering, "What now?" It can be frustrating. Over time, you may be able to improve or even resolve some issues, but you may not be able to improve all of them.

Find the good in where you are today. Sleepless nights can be resolved. Head banging can be healed. And you will figure out how to get your child to wear clothes outside in the winter, I promise, at least for long enough so he or she does not to freeze to death.

Strength Is Your Reward

Your child's autism diagnosis will make you stronger than you ever imagined.

Forget those pit bull mamas, and spare me the hockey moms. I've met many parents of disabled and special needs children, but I've met no one quite like a parent raising a child on the autism spectrum. We fight, we campaign, we try methods that other people call crazy, we even forego our own health, all in the hopes of giving our beautiful, purpose-built children a voice and a future.

Don't fear autism. Instead, learn its ways. Fix the negative behaviors and medical issues that harm your child and the prospects for a good life. Accept the rest of it.

Believe it or not, you can resolve many negative behaviors. The key is to find the root cause of them. You will also be able to dig out your child's strengths to make them shine in ways that the world tells you will not be possible. With our God, nothing is impossible!

Most of all, always empower your child. An autism diagnosis is not the sum total of your child, but it can impact his or her personality, which is as unique and blessed as any other child's.

Avoid the Critics

Because autism is so complex, so heavily debated, and manifests in so many ways, I believe that the best approach to improving your child's life is to "leave no stone unturned." That said, plunking down thousands of dollars for something that worked in one child's life may not be the best route for you or your family, or it may be the one thing that changes everything.

We also live in a day and age where everyone else seems to be an "expert" on what's good for your family. It might take time, but you must ignore the naysayers. You are doing what's best for your child and your family in the best way that you can. That's why it's important to let God lead you. (We'll discuss that in another chapter.)

Personally, we've found the most possibilities in biomedical treatment and bio-individual nutrition. Other modalities that we have tried, some with success, include homeopathy, CBD/cannabis, and herbal remedies.

It's key to learn as much as you can before you try anything. It's also critical to be at peace with your choices. For our family, I refused to put my children on pharmaceuticals because I didn't find any studies of long-term effects of these drugs on a growing brain. I've also seen them wreak havoc on family members, so I was uncertain if my daughter's system could tolerate them without harm.

But that's me and my family, and this is the direction the Lord led us. It might be different for your family, but I encourage you to fully and completely research any type of treatment for your child, including side and long-term effects, case studies, toxicity, and costs.

Whatever treatments you choose, make sure they fit your family, your budget, and your abilities. For example, I've avoided chelating, a procedure that removes mercury from the bloodstream because of its risks, despite seeing benefits to other families. It's a risky procedure if you don't follow an extremely strict protocol, and that's just not a good fit for me.

Treatments of any type can have lifelong effects — good or bad — on your child. Unfortunately, much of the medical community strictly relies on medications and ABA, and may even demonize other protocols, including well-researched nutritional approaches. Keep this in mind while investigating ways you can help your child.

An important resource for you will be other families raising an autistic child who have used interventions to successfully eliminate problematic issues, ranging from sleep challenges to eczema. Don't apologize to anyone for doing the best that you can do with what you know and what you have. Instead, ask the Lord to guide you and give you wisdom to find practical ways to address your child's difficulties.

Hope Is not a Dirty Word

If you ever hear a doctor, psychologist, or other professional say the words, "Your child will never be able to 'fill-in-the-blank'," I recommend you change practitioners immediately. Don't accept defeat. You just have not found the right intervention yet, or you have not done it long enough for it to have an impact. Never give up!

Have a dream for your child based around the person you know he or she is, pursue it, and don't let anyone talk you out of it — school staff, doctor, therapist, health professional, family member, or anyone else. Your child is unique and here for a reason; it's your job to discover it and help him or her find the way. That way will also be the Lord's way! Jesus wants your child to succeed as much as you do. A hopeful outlook is a choice that you can make and pass on to your family, and it will benefit all your children.

The ABCs of Self Care

This road is not easy. It will take a lot out of you. You may start neglecting yourself, foregoing sleep, nutrition, health, and fitness. You might even stop caring how you look or feel. This is a normal adjustment, for a brief time, just like it is directly after bringing home a baby.

The problem is you can't go on like that. Your children need you to be well-rested, strong, and capable. Skipped meals, sleepless nights, and sicknesses that don't heal will drain you even more than your daily responsibilities to your child.

In 2 Corinthians 12:9 (NIV), Paul tells us that God spoke to him, saying, "But He said to me, 'My grace is sufficient for you, for my power is made perfect in weakness.' Therefore I will boast all the more gladly about my weaknesses, so that Christ's power may rest on me."

This is absolutely true, but your weakness does not mean letting yourself go. The Lord wants us to put our best foot forward. God has given us all the time we need in each day to care for our needs as well as those of our children.

Consider the story of Elijah in 1 Kings 19. At the time, Israel was ruled by King Ahab, but the strings of power were pulled by his wife, Queen Jezebel. She was a pagan worshipper and had no respect for the God of Israel nor his prophets. Still, God spoke to His people through the prophet Elijah to Ahab. Elijah performed miracles and demonstrated the Lord's power, executing the false prophets that were loyal to the king.

This only frightened Ahab, and he told his wife what happened. Instead of seeing the light, it made Jezebel furious, and she vowed to kill Elijah. He became frightened and ran for his life.

He was terrified, overwhelmed, and weary. What did he do? Let's pick it up at 1 Kings 19:4, ESV

> But he himself went a day's journey into the wilderness, and came and sat down under a broom tree. And he prayed that he might die, and said, "It is enough! Now, Lord, take my life, for I *am* no better than my fathers!"

Can you imagine? After all he'd done and seen, one of the greatest prophets who ever lived asked God to let him die because he could not go on.

Have you been there? Unable to make it through one more day? It may not just be the challenges your child faces, but a series of terrible things that become piled on: job loss, financial insecurity, divorce, addiction, illness, betrayal, or death. Sometimes the everyday struggles in life just feel impossible when your entire life is being poured into your disabled child.

Elijah must have felt that life was insurmountable because his entire purpose in life put him in jeopardy of execution. He cried out to the Lord to take him away from his burdens.

But God had a different idea:

> Then as he lay and slept under a broom tree, suddenly an angel touched him, and said to him, "Arise and eat." Then he looked, and there by his head was a cake baked on coals, and a jar of water. So he ate and drank, and lay down again. And the angel of the Lord came back the second time, and touched him, and said, "Arise and eat, because the journey is too great for you." So he arose, and ate and drank; and he went in the strength of that food forty days and forty nights as far as Horeb, the mountain of God. — 1 Kings 19:5-8 (NKJV)

And if you continue reading, you'll see that after this, God appointed Elisha as the man to take his place as prophet when the time came. In addition to providing much-needed nourishment and rest, the Lord provided a helper, indicating that Elijah's work would soon be completed.

I think many of us can relate to this. "God, I'm done!" We feel too exhausted to face another day. But in reality, we need to understand that God has appointed us all the hours in a day that we need, *including* caring for ourselves!

Do you need a break? Do you need more sleep? Are you choosing nutritious foods and proper supplements for yourself? Are you on your phone too often, drinking too little water, avoiding walks out in the sun?

Sometimes it's the little things we do for ourselves that add up to big improvements. The Lord wants you to rest and care for your body too!

I want to be clear here. I'm not saying you should take so much time for yourself that your family suffers. I'm saying that you can make small changes to swap the habits you have now for better ones. Create a strategy for better sleep. Start snacking on fruit and vegetables instead of candy or other sweets. Park a little further out in the parking lot to get some walking in the next time you're running errands.

How do we accomplish all this? With God's help of course! Here is a guideline of how you can start taking care of yourself today:

- *Acknowledge* that motherhood has become something much harder than it was intended to be. RIGHT NOW, SAY IT. That's the first step to letting go of guilt and regret.
- *Breathe* deeply three times: Breathe in for 8 seconds, hold your breath for 8 seconds, then slowly exhale for 8 seconds out. This can calm you and focus your mind.
- *Clear* your mind of negativity for 15 to 20 minutes. Let go of stress, worry, or wondering, "How am I going to...?" Invite the Holy Spirit into your mind. Do whatever helps with that: scripture, Christian music, or poetry. And you can also use activities like a hot shower, a cup of tea, a walk in the sun, or a solid workout. Take a short break daily even if it's just 5 or 10 minutes. Try for longer stretches when you can. You need your sanity, your health, and clarity. Adding more "but I have to's" isn't going to get you there. DON'T shirk your responsibilities but DO give your mind and body a much-needed break, even just for a little while.
- *Decompress* by taking another 10 minutes to enjoy yourself at a point during the day. Read a little. Play a game on your phone. Get lost down a Pinterest hole. Read cat humor on Facebook. Just be sure to stop at the end of 10 minutes so you don't get addicted to these distractions.
- *Enjoy* your child. Hug or connect with your children every day, no matter what they're doing. Just let them keep doing it and give them a great big hug—or a small one or a chin tap or head butt if they don't like to be hugged. Use whatever is your nonverbal way to tell your child you love him or her.
- *Feed* your faith. All my sanity comes from my faith in the Lord Jesus to watch over my family and guide my actions. You should be in the Word every day! For me, this habit didn't come overnight. But Bible study (online or in person), church attendance if you can find one that supports your family, small groups that allow you to bring your child, fellowships with Christian brothers and sisters can help you. You can also listen to online sermons, pray the Psalms, read a Proverb a day, and so on. Small bits of scripture daily go a long way to growing your heart for God and getting the respite you need!

Tools to Cope with a Diagnosis

Once you have a diagnosis, take the time to accept and digest it. When you feel comfortable with your new knowledge, it's time to create a plan to help your child. This will happen in stages, but there are several things that have helped me over the years.

In Balance: Routine, Chaos, and Order

I am not good at this. In fact, "spontaneous" could be my middle name. Kids with disabilities, however, require routine to help them thrive. Now, Jesus is a God of order not chaos, that's true, but you must balance out these two things in your life.

If you are like me, inclined toward disorder, then you need to get at least a bit organized. Give your kids predictable schedules to keep them feeling stable and secure.

However, keep in mind that life is rarely stable. Despite the challenges it posed, early on I decided to make sure my kids didn't get so entrenched in routine and order that change would throw them off. Even if you want to keep your kids completely routine-based, remember even changes like school breaks can throw your kids off if you don't find a way to prepare them for it.

One of the best ways to do this is to develop a routine but every now and then, drop it. It's better to do that when you *can* rather than when you *must*. Take opportunities to train your child about chaos and spontaneity. It may not be easy. My daughter hated transitions and changes but over the years she learned to manage it, as we've helped her manage her symptoms and behaviors more easily.

You can also make those changes something your child wants rather than needs. In other words, drop your routine to do something he or she prefers. Then your child will be more open to accepting routine changes.

What I'm suggesting here is a behavioral approach, but not all your child's challenges regarding transition are behavioral. We'll talk about managing transitions in another chapter.

Managing Your Child's Treatment

Children on the autism spectrum often need a lot of management: paperwork, school meetings, applications, therapies, Medicare, etc. Plus, your child can benefit from numerous interventions outside of these types of services: individualized nutrition, supplements, detox protocols, educational services, waivers and funding, and state programs. That means you need to manage lots of deadlines and appointments. You need to keep track of the risks, benefits, costs, and data from all these interventions as well.

To do this, I keep multiple calendars all over my house to make sure I don't miss meetings, days off, events, and other things that are critical for my children. I put notifications on my phone and on my paper calendar.

I also have created sheets and forms to help me coordinate different protocols. If you'd like to track progress or regression over a series of years, you might want to invest in a 10-year calendar too.

You also need a way to keep your spouse and your care providers informed and up to date on whatever they need to know. Create a system where you can easily track all your child's needs. I keep a binder for each of my children to cover all their protocols, therapies, IEPs, and more. In fact, I've developed my own system of worksheets as well that cover every aspect of what parents need. Learn more at https://embracingimperfect. com/autismparents.

Research

Every day, researchers are learning more about autism. The idea that autism is "only" genetic is fading away, as more studies researching environmental factors are being investigated. Today, people believe that environmental factors trigger autism when certain genetic predispositions are in place.

The relatively new science of epigenetics also shows us that everything you do affects the future and health of your genes, and some interventions can impact your child's development in a positive way. Some doctors support this, but others do not. You'll need to do your own medical and scientific research to best help your child.

The learning curve can be challenging, but the blessings are amazing when your child comes away with improved skills or calmer behaviors.

A Spirit of Hope

It's so important to keep and renew the hopes that you have for your child regularly.

There can and will be ups and downs in your emotions and motivations too. In Chapter 2, I'll discuss tips and strategies to keep your faith, optimism, and hope for your child alive and well.

Chapter 2

Looking for Hope from the Only One Who Gives It

And so, Lord, where do I put my hope?
My only hope is in you.
— Psalm 39:7, NLT

I was talking with another mom who is also raising a child on the autism spectrum. We discussed the struggles we face, and let me tell you, they are real.

I've met many moms who have resolved difficult symptoms or behaviors in their autistic children only to have new problems suddenly arise. They come in the form of:

- Regressions
- Unexplained new symptoms
- Illnesses taking an unexpected turn
- New toxic exposure suddenly brought to light, for example, mold in the school or at home

This is the "in between" twilight world that those of us raising autistic children face. Few things are as frightening as getting a note home from school or daycare that reads, "Your daughter bit/hit someone today," or "Your child banged his head intentionally this morning," when you haven't seen that behavior in years.

You suddenly feel like the rug has been pulled out from under you. Your chest constricts, making it hard to breathe, and you experience a sinking feeling. Despair floods your mind, and you begin to second-guess everything:

"Did I mess up her diet?"

"Did I mess up the protocol?"

"Did he catch something?"

"Is this educational setting wrong for her?"

"Was that therapy wrong for him?"

"Is she being bullied or abused and unable to tell me?"

And perhaps the scariest question of all:

"Is this my fault?"

It's natural to be upset. Then you look over at your child and there she is putting her things away, prepping her own snack, and completing her after-school chores. But you have no idea if this is short-lived or if something worse is going to happen.

Perhaps it wasn't just a one-off incident. Maybe your child has gone from great strides forward to deep deficiencies that seem to have come out of nowhere. You are trying to uncover the clues to what may have changed. Was it something too small to detect or was it something major that you should have seen?

The truth is, you may never know. This is the reality of autism, even for those of us who've been through years of a healing journey. Two steps forward, and one, two, or sometimes ten steps back. Detox, stress, life changes, food, and a whole host of things you might not have detected can bring short-or long-term regression. Exposure to new toxins, new situations, and illness can all bring about behavioral, social, and physical symptoms and issues. On and on it goes.

But the enemy of your soul will whisper in your ear that this is all your fault. Satan will repeat as often as it takes to get you to lose faith and hope.

Now, I'm sure that there are parents raising kids who are not on the autism spectrum or without any sort of diagnosis that experience some kind of backslide too. However, the ever-growing community of parents raising children who have a more severe form of autism have a common bond that draws us together.

In fact, there's a unique blessing in raising kids with disabilities: They are totally authentic. They wear their hearts and emotions on their sleeve, they laugh at anything they think is funny, and they'll stop and play or watch things that they enjoy, whether or not it's in their "age range."

It's time to look ahead with hope. Five years can make a big difference in the life of a parent, a child, and a family if you take that time to work with your child and let God lead you down the road He wants your family to explore.

My Journey

When my daughter was little, we were really struggling. She wasn't five years old yet, but we had been through so much. I had no idea how to discipline her, manage her behaviors, or quiet her tantrums. Most of the time, I couldn't uncover her triggers, and when I did, the causes were diverse: the end of certain movies, not being allowed in a room, not being given a treat. Some days she could not help her tantrums, but on others, she used them to manipulate me, my husband, or other caregivers.

At the time, I was exhausted from trying to figure out how to help her. I was also on my own journey to discover the Lord, but I wasn't there yet. I was still stuck in a "why, God, why?" routine as I pondered salvation.

If this is you, you may not realize that there is hope. You may not yet know that your child is eating, drinking, and being exposed to things that may be destroying his or her ability to communicate or smile or laugh. You do not know because no one told you that many children on the spectrum have issues that trigger behaviors. These can include allergies, food and chemical sensitivities, gut health issues, and more.

When my daughter was little, most doctors did not admit that there is a component to autism that is not neurological, behavioral, or genetic. Perhaps you can't understand why your child is not improving despite doing everything recommended by traditional Western medicine: floor time, applied behavior analysis (ABA), well-care check ups, vaccines on schedule, antibiotics for illness, Tylenol and OTC drugs when "needed," three meals a day plus snacks or whatever you can get him or her to eat, and daily vitamins. It turns out that some of those things may have done more harm than good, but you didn't know, and that's okay.

But don't lose hope! God is with you, waiting for the right time and opportunity to show you what to change and when. He led you to read this book *right now*. He is there now watching over your children. I know that now, but I didn't see it back in 2004, when I wrote this about my daughter:

> I love her so much. She has so much awesome potential, and she's maturing her abilities very well this year. But she needs to learn behavior, respect, or as much as a four-year-old can handle. Is that too much to ask, in the last few months before she's five?

It turns out that this is all you need as a parent: love that's just crazy enough to find a solution where others tell you not to look. Love that has broken your heart so badly, you will do *anything* to make your child smile, laugh, or talk. Love that fights for truth, fights for rights fights to help an injured child, and fights to protect her **and** the families of other injured children.

It's just like the love of our perfect Father in Heaven, who loves all His children equally and made the most unconceivable sacrifice to make sure they had a way to enter Heaven too.

This kind of love puts resurrection power inside of you. The Lord sent His only Son to Earth to die for our sins, the ultimate sacrifice to heal our challenges! That is the kind of love you'll need to help your child thrive.

But not every path will be the right one for you. How can you help your child when you are unsure of what God wants you to do? The simple answer is you can't, but you can learn to listen and discern His path for your parenting.

Helping Your Child in Due Time

Ecclesiastes 3:1-8 says that there is a time and a season for everything. The NIV version says:

What do workers gain from their toil? I have seen the burden God has laid on the human race. He has made everything beautiful in its time. He has also set eternity in the human heart; yet no one can fathom what God has done from beginning to end. — Ecclesiastes 3:9-11 (NIV)

Did you catch that? God has made everything beautiful *in its time*. One day your child might break through his or her difficulties and go to college and achieve many things. Or maybe your child will always live with you and cannot hold a job. Who's to say? The work you must do is not finished, but the *hope* you hold in your heart need not diminish no matter what your child's future holds.

That is the kind of hope the Holy Spirit instills in your heart.

There is a time and place for everything, and for me, those times and places came together when I met a friend who attended my daughter's school briefly. She taught me all about the alternatives for treating autism. This completely changed the course of my daughter's life for the better, but I had to be ready to accept that information.

These treatments took financial and emotional commitment. When you are raising a child struggling with the challenges of autism, there are no quick fixes or easy answers. This is a challenging journey, but it can be a path to a brighter future for your child. Not every solution will work, but you will make close, fast, and binding relationships with other parents on this journey, whether healing comes quickly, slowly, or not at all.

That is, unless you choose to measure your child's progress by theirs. Don't waste precious time comparing your child to anyone, nor line up your sorrow against anyone else raising a child with a disability. That will only lead to pain and jealousy. Instead, look for the good in your child. **Every child** comes to this Earth with strengths, talents, and unique, God-given abilities. Never underestimate the worth of things the world doesn't value: a small smile, a big hug, a loyal heart, or a new ability your child acquires even if it's five or ten years after his peers.

In fact, I'd have to say that that the biggest blessing of raising a disabled child has been the joy we've found in simple milestones. To the parents of a typically developing child, these might seem silly. But they will never know the long-awaited joy of a skill that has been delayed, such as the first time they make eye contact, say what they mean, or kissing you. I promise you, it's a feeling that's worth the wait.

Chapter 3

Praying for Your Child

Then children were brought to Him that He might lay his hands on them and pray. The disciples rebuked the people, but Jesus said, "Let the little children come to me and do not hinder them, for to such belongs the kingdom of heaven." And He laid his hands on them and went away. — Matthew 19:13-15, ESV

Raising children with special needs has taught me two big things:
- I cannot do this alone.
- I need to hope for the best without expecting a specific outcome.

Neither one of these is intuitive for me, but I take great strength in the Old Testament (OT) story of Hannah. As told in 1 Samuel 1 and 2, Hannah was one of two wives of Elkanah.* At the start of this story, one wife, Peninnah, who many biblical scholars believe was his second wife, already had many children. However, Hannah was barren. In those days, women who could not have children were treated horribly. It was considered a curse or a punishment from God.

Being unable to bear a child also meant there was no one to take care of you as you grew old. In ancient society, women could not work and required a son to care for them. If a woman did not have a son, she could end up penniless and homeless if she outlived her husband.

This is the state we find poor Hannah in the beginning of 1 Samuel.

Elkanah's family would go to the temple in Shiloh for Passover and the other feasts. Peninnah would mock Hannah for not having children. It was not a nice thing to do, of course, but quite common. After all, the two women likely vied for the attention of their one husband.

One year, Peninnah teased her so viciously that Hannah could not even eat, even though her husband tried to encourage her. After the meal that day, she went to the temple to pray. She fell on her knees begging God to give her a child. She promised to give her child back to God.

She poured out her heart to the Lord, murmuring and begging. She looked so crazy that Eli, the priest, accused her of being drunk. She told him that she was not drunk but asking God to remove her burden of being barren. Eli saw the depths of her pain and blessed her.

After my studies, I've come to believe that having two or more wives was not in God's plan for anyone. Many stories in the Old Testament reveal the problems that come with having multiple wives. This was a choice made by man and not God.

God heard Hannah's prayer. She conceived shortly after the family returned from the temple. Hannah kept her son, Samuel, with her until he was weaned (around age three or four). She kept her promise to the Lord by bringing him back to Eli to be trained as a priest. Samuel, in turn, dedicated his life to the Lord. As for Hannah, she was later blessed with five more children and visited Samuel every year.

What can we learn from this mother of the Bible?

1. Pour the desires and anguish of your heart out to the Lord.

God knows what's in your heart, true, but He wants to hear it *from* you. I know that many look upon the outpouring of problems and despair as "venting" or "anger," but God can bear it. He already knew that Hannah was hurting but it sounds like until the day that she took to her knees in the temple, she had not truly shared her burden with Him. That act changed *everything*. While Eli's blessing may have encouraged her, it was not his actions that touched the Lord but Hannah's.

When you pray for your children, be honest and pour out your anguish to the Lord. When my daughter regressed after puberty, my heart broke. I took it to God, over and over. When I did, the Holy Spirit comforted me in real time, healing my soul and providing a way for me to deal with my struggles.

2. Take comfort in His Word.

If you read further in the story, you'll see that Eli was not the best of priests, but even so, his prayer that the God of Israel grant Hannah's request encouraged her. Eli was meant to be the representative of God on Earth, and even though he had human failings, God still used him to lighten Hannah's load. This was not Eli's doing so much as it was God speaking *through* Eli, as we see Hannah go home and eat. We are told she "was no longer sad."

Today, we don't need an "Eli," we just need a Bible. There have been too many challenges to count with my daughter, and the only thing that has comforted me is hearing from God, through scripture: reading it, memorizing it, holding it in my heart, hearing it in worship music, and from friends sharing scripture. The Bible is an entire book of God's words to comfort us. We can rely on its truth to see us through the most difficult moments of life.

3. Pray with conviction and leave the problem to God.

This is a hard one for me because, as I've mentioned before, I'm a "fixer." God can solve any problem, but He will solve it in a way that shows His glory. Hannah's painful years of being barren made her subsequent pregnancies a way to glorify God. Only He could change that path for her.

However, when we pray, we must not doubt. James writes about asking God for wisdom:

> But let him ask in faith, with no doubting, for he who doubts is like a wave of the sea driven and tossed by the wind. For let not that man suppose that he will receive anything from the Lord; he is a double-minded man, unstable in all his ways. — James 1:6-7

Pray for your whatever is on your heart; pray for whatever you want for your children. Healing? Yes! Recovery? Yes! Salvation? Always! Academic success, speech impediment gone, social behaviors fixed, no more OCD? Yes, all that and more!!

4. God always answers the prayers of the faithful.

Okay, so let's be real: Hannah suffered, but in the end, she was lucky. You and I know it. Not all of us will get the answers we want, as Hannah did. When you've broken down numerous times and still don't see recovery or improvement in your child, you might wonder where your answers are.

It's not that God won't answer your prayer. He will one way or another, and that other way may not be what you want. It might not be the way you imagined. In fact, you may get what you want in a way you didn't want and don't think you can handle. Or, you may not be prepared for it yet so you have to wait longer.

We don't know how many years Hannah suffered, but it was enough to break her spirit. What we do know is the Lord had a purpose through her trial.

- God wanted her first child, Samuel, to serve Him as a priest and a prophet to Israel's first kings.
- Her gratitude and faith caused God to bless her with many more children after that.
- Her story is memorialized for all time as a picture of a faithful mom and servant to God, to encourage mothers throughout history.

God prepared a different and ultimately better road for Hannah, and He will do the same for you. He will answer your prayers, and He will give you the strength to accept that answer, even if the answer is "no."

5. Give your heartfelt thanks to the Lord when your prayer is answered.

Samuel is an especially important Biblical figure. He is the last judge of Israel, a prophet, a priest, a counselor, and a true man of God. There are two books of the Bible named after him. He was the advisor of Israel's first two kings, Saul and David, and is mentioned in the list of Old Testament heroes in Hebrews 11.

Long before Hannah had more children, she brought Samuel to the temple, which was not near her home. She dropped off her preschooler, not expecting to see him for at least a year, and what did she do next?

She worshipped God. She publicly thanked God for answering her prayers and giving her a child exactly when she had to give him up for good. Her prayer was not a short one but a whole ten verses, an entire page of worship for the goodness of the Lord.

She sings a song of worship in 1 Samuel 2:1-10, and after that the very next line is, "Then Elkanah and Hannah returned home to Ramah without Samuel." I can't even imagine how difficult that journey home was for her. At the same time, I think Hannah, in her heart, knew that Samuel would be a great man of God. I think this blessed her and gave her joy despite her loss. The question is how do we find joy when we give up things for our kids, including dreams for the future we once thought they would have?

What We Learn from Hannah

Hannah's outpouring of her heart, trust in the Lord, dedication of her child, and song of praise are lessons all parents can learn from, especially those of us raising kids with challenges, difficulties, and special needs. However, I don't want you think of what Hannah did as making a "deal" with God. That is a trap you should resist.

Pray for your children but do not offer something in return other than your thanks. Give your child to God out of your own free will and not in exchange for an answered prayer or a wish list. Simply ask for your dreams and hopes for your child. That's what He wants, and He will be faithful to answer.

Finally, when you pray, do so as the Bible instructs: without willful sin or worry in your heart, without anything against your neighbor, with an open heart and clear conscience after confessing, and repenting of what's weighing on your soul.

A good pattern of prayer is "ACTS":

- Adoration: Praise God for who He is, the perfect Father, whose faithful and unconditional love will see you through.
- Confession: Search your soul and ask God to convict you of your sins before making requests.
- Thanksgiving: Thank Him for the blessings He's provided you, including your precious autistic child.
- Supplication: Now it's time for prayer requests. Pray for those nearest and dearest (husband and children) first and for yourself last. Ask for God's help in teaching you how to pray. A great way to pray is by reading scriptures. For example, Psalms and Proverbs are chockfull of verses we can turn into prayers. Here are some additional scriptures on prayer:
  - 1 Thessalonians 5:16-18
  - Philippians 4:6-7
  - 1 John 5:14
  - Mark 11:24
  - Hebrews 4:16

Chapter 4

The (Spiritual) Causes of Autism

Therefore, just as sin entered the world through one man, and death through sin, and in this way death came to all people, because all sinned.
— Romans 5:12, NIV

Why does your child have autism? This question has plagued parents for decades. There are several perspectives. Personally, my opinion is that autism requires a genetic predisposition that makes your child's system overly sensitive to environmental influences, such as toxins. This, in turn, disrupted development and/or function of different systems, such as autoimmune function or brain chemistry.

Some experts in the field believe that autism is part of autoimmune dysfunction. Others argue against this and claim that it is merely a genetic condition, which leads to a person's brain being wired differently. There is science on both sides, but I believe that the evidence is better on one side than the other.

There is a chance that one day we will know all the causes of autism. I hope and pray that is the case. However, there is another side to all this: the spiritual dimension. Why do some people have severe and debilitating cases of autism?

One simple answer: Sin. I'm not talking about your sin or your child's. While sin can have consequences, it does not cause illness, according to Jesus. (Read John 9:1-5.)

Here, I am talking about a condition that prevents normal function. People with profound autism have numerous social, behavioral, intellectual, and even medical challenges that make it difficult or impossible to do everyday things. Speech disability, motor dysfunction, gut issues, and a variety of challenges that severely autistic people can have make it difficult for them to hold a job, maintain relationships, or even live on their own safely.

I think you'd agree that this makes for a significant issue. According to the CDC, autism prevalence has gone up from 1 in 150 in the year 2000 to 1 in 36 in 2012.[1] While some contribute this increase to better diagnosis, others see a lack of evidence for that fact so we don't know for sure why there has been such an increase. But we do know this is a crisis.

1. https://www.cdc.gov/ncbddd/autism/data.html

Any condition that robs you of your ability to live an abundant life, or even to make a clear conscious decision whether or not to follow Jesus, is not from the Lord but has its roots in the sinfulness of humanity.

The Impact of Sin

Sin came into this world through one man, Adam. The Bible tells us that before Adam and Eve sinned, they lived in harmony with God along with all of nature. Whether or not you believe in a literal translation of the creation story, the point is the same: We began as a sinless creation, but our propensity to choose fleshly desires over the goodness that God offers us prevents us from entering Heaven without a mediator. We cannot live sinless lives, free from harm and death.

We come into this world, at first, sinning unwittingly but eventually moving our way toward willful actions. The early chapters of Genesis show us that the sins of humanity also grow bigger after humans are expelled from the garden of Eden. Adam and Eve's sin was simple disobedience, but their son was the first person to commit murder.

The more we sin, the more harm we do to ourselves, our fellow humans, the world at large. History is rife with heinous examples of how humankind justified sins. Collecting taxes? Add a surcharge to skim the profits. Need people to work for you? Have slaves instead. Unhealthy baby? Leave them to die.

Over time, sin led to disease and other maladies. Incest brought disabilities. Promiscuity brought sexually transmitted diseases. Greed brought tainted medicines. Indulgence brought drug addiction and sexual sins. Does sin breed death? Yes, and disease along with it.

While many debate the cause of autism, the fact that we are dealing with so many children in crisis is because we live in a fallen world. In a perfect world, children would not have gut health issues, learning disabilities, self-injurious behaviors, aggression, epilepsy, and the host of other behavioral, medical, and social challenges that present alongside autism.

Jesus Heals Our Sinful Nature

The good news is that, as believers, we are redeemed of our sins through one man, Jesus. We don't have to be upset about the causes of autism, but we do have to acknowledge that there is only one way out of sin and suffering. There is nothing we have to do except freely embrace God's gift of grace through the sacrifice of His one and only Son as payment for any and all sins we commit. Once we do that, salvation, redemption, and eternal life are ours, and nothing can take that away.

After that, the Holy Spirit will work on our hearts to change us. I wish I could tell you that this road will be paved with nothing but highs. When new Christians are first saved, they often experience joy like they are walking on air and nothing can touch them. But it doesn't last long because once we are redeemed, Satan sets his laser-like focus on us to take away our joy.

But that's okay. The truth is that life's difficulties shape our character and make us more Christ-like. The challenges of raising an autistic child may not lessen when you walk with Jesus, but He is ready to carry your burdens for you every single day.

To be clear, I am in no way implying that eliminating your sins will eliminate your child's autism diagnosis. There may be steps you can take to help your child live a better life. There may be nothing more you can do or nothing that is working like you've seen it work on other children.

I can guarantee, however, that walking closely with the Lord Jesus will bless you, your child, and your family in ways you cannot even imagine right now!

Let's explore some of the situations we face as autism parents and how we can handle them with Jesus on the throne of our hearts. We'll start with our own sins.

Chapter 5

Dealing with Sin in Your Heart: Anger

And I am sure of this, that he who began a good work in you will bring it to completion at the day of Jesus Christ. — Philippians 1:6, ESV

Once you are saved, the Lord will not leave you alone. He has sent the Holy Spirit into your heart to act as your navigator and guide. The promptings of the Spirit will help you discern right from wrong, good from evil, and trustworthy from unreliable.

Before we go further, I want to make sure you know that in this discussion of sinful emotions, I'm talking about a condition of the heart. Anger, depression, and other harmful thoughts can also be side effects of certain drugs or substance abuse, chemical imbalances, mental crises, or other challenges that are out of your control. Those are not the difficulties I'm talking about here. Rather, this covers the willful choices of sin.

It takes time to become more Christ-like, and the process will not end until you are called to Heaven. Corinthians 3:18 says, "And we all, with unveiled faces, beholding the glory of the Lord, are being transformed into the same image from one degree of glory to another. For this comes from the Lord who is the Spirit." This process is slow for our own protection. In His great mercy, the Lord will not reveal and help you work through all your sins at once. That would be overwhelming, and our sense of despair at our own depravity would set us back.

Instead, God takes you by the hand to help you work through the specific elements that you need for the upcoming days, weeks, and months or even the next few years. As you learn to follow His will more closely, you may discover that He has healed the very thing you needed in order to cope with a situation or minister to someone else. I'm going to go through a few of these sins to help you see what God is asking of you.

The Dangers of Anger

In the Bible, Jesus says:

> But I tell you that anyone who is angry with a brother or sister will be subject to judgment. Again, anyone who says to a brother or sister, "Raca," is answerable to the court. And anyone who says, "You fool!" will be in danger of the fire of hell. — Matthew. 5:22, NIV ("Raca" is an insult.)

First and foremost, anger over your child's diagnosis is something you need to deal with. One of the reasons is that you may be falsely assuming that your anger is "righteous." It may have started out that way, but has it morphed into something else? Or is the root of this emotion anger at God? That is a very dangerous road, as I learned.

When my daughter turned seven, I became convinced that my child had injuries that had been aggravated by toxins and our doctors had knowingly turned a blind eye to that issue. In 2015, I saw that my older daughter, Amelia, who has Down syndrome, was likely injured as well. As the years went by and I did more research, I saw more evidence that damaging things were happening to kids all over the country as a result of how their doctors were treating them. The forces of greed and complacency had allowed this evil to grow.

But back in 2012, I was still new to this idea, and I thought it gave me the right to righteous anger. It is true that true evil perpetrated on innocents should make us angry. There is nothing ungodly about that.

The problem comes after our initial reaction. Do we hang on to that anger? I wrote a blog post about my "righteous" anger. While I might have been on the right track at first, I now believe that I wrote that post so my anger could perpetually live on my blog.

It's difficult to have an objective perspective on how much my anger actually blinded me, but I have seen other parents who are wrapped so tightly that they cannot let go of their pain and agony. As humans, we struggle to understand where and when righteous anger becomes sinful anger. Can you recognize the difference? It's not easy to discern.

And there is a difference. The Bible identifies three kinds of anger:

- Righteous or justifiable anger
- General anger
- Fury, more commonly called rage

Do you know what kind of anger is in your heart? Let's look in the Bible for answers.

Righteous Anger

There are two key stories that feature justifiable anger in the Bible that I'd like to mention. I'm going through them in order.

Moses: Anger over a False God

In Exodus 32, we find the Israelites wandering through the desert after the Lord freed them from the hands of the Egyptians, who were working them to death. Rather than being grateful to God, these newly freed people complained and whined to Moses, their leader. Then God called Moses to come up the mountain to give him the basis of Biblical law, the Ten Commandments.

As the people impatiently waited for him to return, they asked Aaron, Moses' brother and the first Israelite priest, to make them an idol to worship. He took their gold and cast an idol of a calf. They then worshipped it as the god who brought them out of Egypt.

When Moses came down from the mountain, he saw his people dancing and worshipping the calf. Of course, this was an affront to God and clearly violated the commandments that God had just handed him. In Exodus 32:19-20, we see that "his anger burned and he threw the tablets out of his hands, breaking them to pieces at the foot of the mountain. And he took the calf the people had made and burned it in the fire; then he ground it to powder, scattered it on the water and made the Israelites drink it."

Moses' anger is justified because the people have turned their back on the God who has done so much for them. They preferred a false idol to not only worship but also thank for bringing them out of Egypt.

This story is hard to understand because we know that God did great miracles to help Israelites escape the Egyptians, like parting the Red Sea. However, we must remember that the Israelites lived in Egypt 400 years. The pagan idols of the Egyptians had permeated their own culture. They may have even mingled Yahweh and these false gods. They may have thought that Moses died and felt they needed to "do something."

Moses was righteously furious in this situation because these people have seen the hand of God directly, and his brother was responsible as the high priest to protect them from their pagan tendencies. He should have known better than to give into their demands. Moses was only gone for forty days, but the Israelites had waited for centuries to be saved from the Egyptians. Could they not see that Yahweh alone had accomplished this? Instead, they were blinded by impatience and lost their way in just a few short weeks.

This story holds important lessons for each of us as we examine the roots of our anger. Does your anger stem from someone violating God's laws or putting a false idol before Him, especially when people should know better? Or does it come from your frustration and impatience in feeling powerless while waiting on the Lord?

I know that for me, that second reason is true more often than I'd like to admit. Even if we know that God's timing is best, doubting and questioning while waiting can lead us to sin. Impatience and focusing on the problem, beyond looking for Spirit-led solutions, can open a foothold for Satan to come in and sow seeds of doubt.

Jesus: Anger at Religious Leaders

In Matthew 21:12-13, Jesus shows what's important to Him:

Jesus entered the temple courts and drove out all who were buying and selling there. He overturned the tables of the moneychangers and the benches of those selling doves. "It is written," He said to them, "My house will be called a house of prayer, but you are making it a den of robbers.'"

33

This story is also recounted in a slightly different fashion in John 2:

> When the Jewish Passover was near, Jesus went up to Jerusalem. In the temple courts He found men selling cattle, sheep, and doves, and moneychangers seated at their tables. He made a whip out of cords and drove all from the temple courts, both sheep and cattle. He poured out the coins of the moneychangers and overturned their tables. To those selling doves He said, "Get these out of here! How dare you turn My Father's house into a marketplace!"
>
> His disciples remembered that it is written: "Zeal for Your house will consume Me." — John 2: 13-17

In this much-misinterpreted story, Jesus showed His disdain when people disrespect His Father. The moneychangers were located in the outer courts, which was an area set aside for converted Jews to worship God. Only people who were born Jewish were allowed inside the temple. while those who had converted had to worship in the outer court. Instead, it had been set up as a type of marketplace.

When the Jewish people came into the temple, they were required to give an offering in cash. Many also came to make a sacrifice. To facilitate this, these so-called "moneychangers" had set up tables in the temple. They were supposed to make it easier for the people to make an offering. They did this by exchanging the Roman currency that everyone used for the Jewish coins, shekels, which were the only kind the temple would accept. They also sold birds and other animals for worshippers to offer a sacrifice.[1]

However, these sellers were often dishonest. They charged a fee for exchanging the currency and overcharged for the sacrificial animals. Of course, merchants were not allowed inside the temple, but they had little respect for the worship of those who converted.

These businessmen used a place that God Himself commanded was to be a holy place of worship in order to make money off Gentiles who wanted to honor God. Thus, Jesus quotes two Old Testament passages: "house of prayer" is from Isaiah 56:7, and "den of thieves" is from Jeremiah 7:11. Jesus was rightfully angry that the moneychangers had used God's holy temple for profit, sullying its true purpose.

In both cases above, Jesus and Moses got angry when God was disrespected. His laws and purposes were forsaken, and sin took over. The Israelites of Moses' time saw God walk before them, and yet turned their backs to worship an idol. The moneychangers in Jesus' time took advantage of worshippers to profit from their devotion to God.

Any time we see God's will violated and His name sullied, we can and should feel righteous anger, but it is our responsibility to fight the temptation to let that anger burn. You must turn it over to God and ask Him what He requires you to do about it, if anything. He will guide you to the best actions.

1. https://www.gotquestions.org/money-changers-in-the-Bible.html

Let's look at the other types of anger and see why we need to be careful with this emotion.

General Anger: Moses, Numbers 20:2-12

The next example again deals with Moses, clearly one of the most famous figures in the Old Testament. Born to a royal family and growing through deeply flawed beginnings, we see that by the time of his death, Moses was a man wholly devoted to the Lord. But when I studied his life in detail, it came as a great surprise that he paid a remarkably high price for a sin that does not seem like a big deal to most of us.

The story takes place in Numbers 20. The Israelites were still wandering through the desert after having been released from the hands of the Egyptians. They were meant to enter the land God promised them, but their sin and disbelief angered the Lord. Instead of gratitude for their freedom, they bitterly complained about life in the desert. In this story, they had run out of water, and once again as a people, they turned to anger rather than to the Lord:

> Now there was no water for the community, and the people gathered in opposition to Moses and Aaron. They quarreled with Moses and said, "If only we had died when our brothers fell dead before the Lord! Why did you bring the Lord's community into this wilderness, that we and our livestock should die here? Why did you bring us up out of Egypt to this terrible place? It has no grain or figs, grapevines or pomegranates. And there is no water to drink!"
> —Numbers 20:2-5, NIV

I can't even imagine how frustrated Moses and Aaron must have been by then. They were released from backbreaking daily labor under the whip, from being forced to meet impossible quotas, yet here the people were whining about *pomegranates*?

By this point in the book of Numbers, the Israelites had already complained about their hardships: the lack of meat, being stuck in the wilderness, and having to face giant people in the land. They had questioned Moses' leadership capabilities, as well as God's judgment in making him their leader. Each time, God either blessed or punished them, showing both infinite mercy and divine wrath. He desperately wanted His people to trust Him even in the most difficult trials.

Sound familiar?

But the Israelites weren't done grumbling yet. In spite of this, Moses and Aaron did their best to help the people:

> Then Moses and Aaron went from the presence of the assembly to the entrance of the Tent of Meeting. They fell facedown, and the glory of the Lord appeared to them. And the Lord said to Moses, "Take the staff and assemble the congregation. You and your brother Aaron are to speak to the rock while they watch, and it will pour out its water. You will bring out water from the rock and provide drink for the congregation and their livestock." Numbers 20: 6-8, ESV

Despite their hard hearts, God still provided. The problem was that Moses was still at the end of his rope with the people. Because of his frustration, he did things a little differently than what God had requested.

> So, Moses took the staff from the Lord's presence, just as He had commanded. Then Moses and Aaron gathered the assembly in front of the rock, and Moses said to them, "Listen now, you rebels, must we bring you water out of this rock?" Then Moses raised his hand and struck the rock twice with his staff, so that a great amount of water gushed out, and the congregation and their livestock were able to drink. — Numbers 20:9-11, NIV

Now, I know it's hard to see, Moses had actually *disobeyed* the Lord here. God had told him to speak to the rock, but Moses hit it with the staff. Not only that, but he says, "must we bring you water out of this rock?" It's hard to tell whether that "we" meant Moses and God, or Moses and Aaron, but either way, Moses is taking some of the credit for what only God can do.

What seems like a small thing is not really. You see, the Israelites, as mentioned in the last section, had spent many years surrounded by the influence of the Egyptians. When Moses had confronted Pharaoh months earlier to set the Jewish people free and God sent the plagues on the Egyptians, the king had his magicians do their own magic tricks, which the people believed. (We don't know if he used Satanic forces or if their magic was just sleight of hand, but either way, the people believed they were seeing magic.)

They might have seen tricks brought about by a "magic staff." They did see Moses turn his staff into a serpent (Exodus 7:10). His staff was also used to bring on some of the plagues (Exodus 7:20-21, 8:6, 8;17, 9:23, and 10:13). However, all of those things were done for Pharaoh's benefit and in the name of God. For example, in Exodus 7:17, God instructed Moses to directly tell Pharaoh that He was causing the first plague.

As mentioned above, in Numbers 20:10, Moses said: "Listen, you rebels, must we bring you water out of this rock?" just before striking the rock, instead of telling them that God was bringing the water. But what happens next?

> But the Lord said to Moses and Aaron, "Because you did not trust Me to show My holiness in the sight of the Israelites, you will not bring this assembly into the land I have given them." — Numbers 20:12, (Berean)

Moses took some credit, rather than letting the people see God's holiness. As punishment, he was not allowed to enter the promised land, and although he saw it before his death, he never stepped foot in it.

The consequences, from our perspective, seem overly harsh. *Well, we think, Moses was at his wit's end! How else was he supposed to react? It was a slip up brought on by frustration.*

And I can't fault you for thinking that, but here's what I do want you to think about.

When was the last time in your home that you got so angry you "lost it"? You know what I mean: yelling, screaming, cursing. Or becoming the silent type who freezes out your family for hours. Did you just get angry for a moment, or did you take it too far even though you knew you should just let it go?

We've all been there. You wanted to stop, but your pride got in the way and you kept going. Afterward, you probably felt like you didn't even deserve forgiveness and had no idea how to apologize. After all, you knew you were wrong, and you didn't stop.

This is the kind of sin that Moses got stuck in. Moses had actually seen part of God Himself. He glowed from being in the presence of God's glory when he was on the mountain with the Lord for forty days, getting the Ten Commandments. God had been talking to him directly for decades at this point. Moses absolutely *knew* that any and all power he saw came from God alone.

He also knew that he was speaking on behalf of the Lord to a distracted, disheartened group of people who struggled with their faith repeatedly. The Lord Himself calls them "stiff-necked" (Exodus 32:9). According to GotQuestions.org,[2] this word means "to be obstinate and difficult to lead." And yet, God had appointed Moses specifically to shepherd this flock. And God always equips those whom He calls upon to be up to the task, no matter how difficult it is.

And yet, Moses lost his temper so badly, that he allowed the people to think the "magic" water was his doing rather than the Lord's provision. For months they had been questioning Moses' leadership and authority. Moses' act was more than just a sin of anger and rage; it was pride, buried down deep in his heart.

In this passage, he falters so badly that he pays the highest price. Imagine the great leader of the exodus not being able to step foot into the Promised Land! Yet, we know that God is just, and it's through this lens that we must view this judgment.

None of us are Moses, but we hopefully aren't like the Israelites either. The deeper you go with your faith in Christ, the more responsibility is expected of you. This means you will bear the consequences of those willful sins that you know you should not be doing while you're in the midst of them.

It may be time to reconsider your anger, even if initially you thought it was justified. The fact is that righteous anger doesn't stay static. It either becomes God-directed action, or it mutates into sin. You can't have both. In the first story, Moses was right to be angry about the people worshipping a statue made of their gold, but he didn't stay angry long enough to sin or disobey God.

In the second story, Moses' anger had nothing to do with God and everything to do with his pride and frustration. And while God's discipline

2.   https://www.gotquestions.org/Bible-stiff-necked.html

was harsh, Moses was blessed to have it. Who knows what price he would have paid had his anger festered into rage?

Rage: Genesis 2b-16

There is no better example in the Bible of rage than way back in the beginning of the book of Genesis. Genesis 4 is a compelling story of how unchecked anger can turn into rage.

Adam and Eve had two sons, Cain first, followed by Abel. They each had different jobs:

> Now Abel kept flocks, and Cain worked the soil. In the course of time Cain brought some of the fruits of the soil as an offering to the Lord. And Abel also brought an offering—fat portions from some of the firstborn of his flock. The Lord looked with favor on Abel and his offering, but on Cain and his offering He did not look with favor. So, Cain was very angry, and his face was downcast. — Genesis 4:26-5, NIV

Right off the bat, Cain is angry. Is it because he was the older brother and thought Abel was showing off? Was he annoyed that he had to give away part of the fruits of his labors?

We don't know why precisely Cain was angry, but he seems to blame God. These verses clearly show that Abel didn't just bring "some" of the fruits of his labor like Cain did; he gave the *very* best of what he had. This implies that Cain kept his choicest crop and offered God what he didn't want to keep. We can't know for sure, but it is possible he gave the bruised, dented, and damaged produce instead of the best.

Whatever actually happened, Cain did not have the right mindset. The Lord answered him right away:

> Then the Lord said to Cain, "Why are you angry? Why is your face downcast? If you do what is right, will you not be accepted? But if you do not do what is right, sin is crouching at your door; it desires to have you, but you must rule over it." — Genesis 4:6-7, NIV

God tells Cain what he did wrong and how to make things right. Instead, Cain chooses to do play the victim.

> Now Cain said to his brother Abel, "Let's go out to the field." While they were in the field, Cain attacked his brother Abel and killed him. — Genesis 4:8, NIV

To us, it sounds like that escalated quickly! However, I'm willing to bet that the anger, which is so apparent throughout this chapter, had festered into rage over many years. Now, Cain is not just angry with Abel. He's also angry at God. God knows his sin:

> The Lord said, "What have you done? Listen! Your brother's blood cries out to me from the ground. Now you are under a curse and driven from the ground, which opened its mouth to receive your

brother's blood from your hand. When you work the ground, it will no longer yield its crops for you. You will be a restless wanderer on the earth."

Cain said to the Lord, "My punishment is more than I can bear. Today you are driving me from the land, and I will be hidden from your presence; I will be a restless wanderer on the earth, and whoever finds me will kill me."

But the Lord said to him, "Not so; anyone who kills Cain will suffer vengeance seven times over." Then the Lord put a mark on Cain so that no one who found him would kill him. So, Cain went out from the Lord's presence and lived in the land of Nod, east of Eden.
—Genesis 4:10-16, NIV

As we can see, anger and rage can have long-ranging, damaging consequences. Cain was given a difficult and lifelong punishment, but the Lord protected him from murder. This shows two things:

- God showed great mercy in dealing with even the first murderer. He saw Cain's fear and comforted him that he would be protected.
- God required a punishment. Cain can't get out of this with an early or quick death. He is meant to live his life under this burden, something he will never forget. Sometimes God does this because after a time, a person will repent because of the guilt they are feeling.

While I hope that none of us would ever seriously consider murder, we must view this story in terms of our own sinful actions. How do we live our lives so that we don't suffer the consequences of our actions? Even though the Lord is just and merciful, we can set things into motion that we cannot escape or take hurtful actions that we cannot take back.

As parents, most of us have experienced that. Have you ever unreasonably lost your temper in front of your children? I'm ashamed to say that has happened to me. I recall a day when I was tired, stressed, and couldn't find something my child had hidden. Rather than take it to God, I yelled and said something I truly regretted.

I was so ashamed afterward because I knew my words had been indelibly carved on my daughters' souls—both of them, even though I only yelled at one. This is the true price we pay for anger as parents: lasting damage to our kids. If we look hard enough, we can see it.

Turns out I don't have to look hard at all. Both my girls will self-talk all the nasty things I say after I yell.

How do your kids call out your angry reactions?

Another issue this story deals with is victimhood, a mindset that is truly destructive. Can you hear the whine in Cain's voice as he said, "I don't know. Am I my brother's keeper?"

On some level, he might have been thinking; *Sure, I killed him, but he provoked me! It's not my fault! I did what I was supposed to do! Why does he get all the good stuff?*

We know that this is all Cain's fault. He was jealous of his brother and acted, then pretended he didn't know that Abel was dead. And when God passed judgment on him, he went further into victimhood: "My punishment is more than I could bear."

Yet, God specifically told him before he killed Abel to stop walking in sin!

Have you ever had that happen to you? Ignoring the Spirit prompting you to stop, even when you knew that doing the next thing was a step too far.

We have all done this before. When we look at the Bible, we are shocked at the sins of holy people, like Moses. But Satan will tempt us to sin when we put on self-righteousness or victimhood. We need to break this cycle. And that starts with recognizing the form and shape of our anger.

How to Discern Anger

While it's easy to see rage, how can we spot anger within us before it grows into something more dangerous? The answers are in scripture. Let's compare and contrast justified anger from sinful anger.

Sinful Anger	Righteous Anger
Is selfish (James 4:1-2)	Is concerned with things that anger or disrespect God (John 2:17)
Smolders (Matt 5:22)	Acts for justice (Luke 19:45-46)
Turns into rage (Gen 4:7)	Does not grow into sin (Eph. 4:26)
Comes on quickly, is passionate, produces strife (Proverbs 30:33).	Rises slowly in response to things that anger God (James 1:19-20)
Matures into sin and death (Gen 4:8)	Is surrendered to God and His will, knows that God's justice is supreme (Rom. 12:19)
Provides an opportunity for the devil to put a foothold in your life (Eph. 4:26-27)	Inspires change and Christian leadership, promotes actions that glorify God (Psalm 7:11)

How to Handle Anger

At the onset of angry emotions, there are steps you can take to diffuse your rage. First, determine if what you are feeling is sinful anger or righteous anger. This can take some time. Because of our pride, we always want to believe that our anger is righteous, but we know that is rarely true.

Jesus only showed anger a few times. More frequently, he showed patience, love, and forgiveness. Turn to God and ask Him to help you discern the root of your anger: selfishness or the Holy Spirit? You might be surprised.

After praying, turn to scripture. God will speak to you about your anger. Here is what the Bible says about handling anger:

- A hot-tempered person stirs up conflict, but the one who is patient calms a quarrel. — Proverbs 15:18, NIV
- Better a patient person than a warrior, one with self-control than one who takes a city. — Proverbs 16:32, NIV

And about dealing with your children:

- Parents,* do not exasperate your children; instead, bring them up in the training and instruction of the Lord. — Ephesians 6:4, NIV

This is an interesting turnabout! *We* are not to exasperate *them*? In the New Living Translation version, it reads: "Do not provoke your children to anger by the way you treat them."

God wants us to understand that since we are the adults, we have to act like it. When your kids are angry, whose fault is it? Have they lost their temper because you screamed? Did you do something impetuous or irreversible, like break their toy? Or did you use words and profanities to cut through them?

Ephesians 6:4 instructs us that we must discipline our children in a way that does not anger them. Kids never like discipline and may grumble, complain, or get angry in the moment. That's human, but your demeanor when correcting them is critical. Be calm when you are talking with them.

Often, we may be tempted to dole out harsh punishment that may be difficult or impossible to manage. Telling a nonverbal child, "No iPad for a month!" is cruel and restrictive if that's his or her only means of communication, but in the heat of an argument you can make mistakes like that. And if you walk back a punishment, you will look weak and indecisive in your child's eyes. That can cost you their respect.

Give yourself time to cool down and ask God to forgive and soothe your anger before determining how to correct or discipline your child. Use a level head to appropriate action that he or she will understand.

As parents, we are all subject to anger from time to time. We must take extra care not to let this emotion cause us to say or do things that harm our kids in ways they cannot communicate.

Original text says "fathers" but it applies to mothers as well.

Chapter 6

Dealing with Sin in Your Heart: Despair

But we have this treasure in jars of clay to show that this all-surpassing power is from God and not from us. We are hard pressed on every side, but not crushed; perplexed, but not in despair; persecuted, but not abandoned; struck down, but not destroyed. — 2 Corinthians 4:7-12, NIV

Despair. It creeps up on you when things continually and repeatedly don't go as you expected. When your child is not healing. When nothing improves despite your best efforts. When school fails your child, therapies are ineffective, medical issues build up, and bills pile up. When your marriage is in trouble, your job is gone, your nonautistic child is struggling, or the price of everything has gone up considerably. Whatever challenging circumstances you find yourself in, hopelessness is never far behind.

And when you lose hope, despair creeps in. Paul talks about this in 2 Corinthians 4:8 when he says about Christians that, "We are afflicted in every way, but not crushed; perplexed, but not driven to despair..." We may be confused about things, but if we trust Jesus, we can avoid the despair that we can experience when we don't know what to do.

But trusting the Lord is not easy when you cannot see a way out or you thought healing was promised to you years ago and you don't see it at all. I can still recall the disappointment I felt after seeing a highly recommended specialist whose treatment plan did nothing to improve my daughter's challenges, despite months of trying.

There are other worldly actions that can lead us to despair. There's no easy fix, but you can strengthen your walk with the Lord by taking these steps with His help.

Avoid Comparison

I remember the time that a local mom talked about her son, who was in kindergarten. He had autism and was unbelievably intelligent. He had savant level skills in many areas, like vocabulary. He was fully verbal and very engaged. As I watched him, my heart broke for my own daughter, who had none of those skills despite having the same diagnosis. I watched with envy as he effortlessly chatted with me on a host of facts. I went home and cried.

Then I realized that I was indulging in comparison, which is the root of envy. It also smacks of ingratitude. Weren't the children the Lord provided me with enough? Why was I complaining when they had brought so much joy into my life? Parenting disabled children taught me to rely on the Lord. It is one of the main reasons I follow Him so closely to this day. While my kids have their struggles, I learned a lot on this journey, and I am stronger and more faithful to God as a result of it.

Years later, Zoe had her own savant moments when she excelled at advanced math. I cherished it, and though it did not last, I have never forgotten that it was there. I still have faith that if the Lord wills it, those abilities will return.

Since then, I make sure I see her for exactly who she is. Intellectual ability no longer has the high value that I once placed on it. It was a false idol I had built for myself that hurt my relationships with my children. God has helped me tear it down over the years.

Now when I look at my children, I see strength, vibrancy, joy, and heart. I see how they have a place and a purpose in this world—whether or not they can do math. I revel in the joy they bring me, and it is plenty, even on the most difficult days.

So now it's your turn: Are you comparing your child to his or her peers who are performing at or above "typically developing" levels? Are you focusing on his struggles, her weaknesses, and your worries? Or are you seeing the treasure of a child that the Lord Himself specifically designed for you to raise to adulthood?

Psalms 127:3 (NIV) says, "Children are a heritage from the Lord, offspring a reward from Him." It doesn't say "some children." It doesn't say "healthy children." It means *all* children. The Lord loves your children. By helping your child and trusting the Lord's will, raising your child can bring you joy, peace, and faith. Pray for the Lord to help you to see your child for exactly who he or she is and ask for guidance to help raise them to be the adults the Lord purposed them to be.

Build Trust in the Lord

One of the reasons you may be struggling is because you don't trust the Lord enough. I know because I have been there regularly. In fact, if I'm honest, it's something I need to remind myself of every single week.

Your level of trust in the Lord will be tested over and over as you grow in your Christian walk. God wants to be the center of your life. Jesus needs to sit on the throne of your heart and navigate every action of your life.

But that doesn't happen overnight. Recently, we were faced with nearly losing our home. My husband had been unemployed, and despite our best efforts at job hunting and bringing in side hustles, we could not pay our bills in full. Even getting additional help did not work.

So, we prayed. We asked everyone we knew to pray as well. Weeks turned into months, and I wondered where we would live. Our mortgage cost less than local rental rates. Losing our home meant we'd have to upend our entire lives and move away from our church and the school district we loved. The kids were struggling enough, and we had anxiety. What would happen? I wanted badly to trust the Lord, but I couldn't see how this would not set back the spiritual ground we had gained.

At the last possible moment, we were saved. My husband got a job—a permanent position for the first time in years—and we were notified about how our church could help us. We took the help and the job. God was faithful to the outcome that actually glorified Him the most. It even led to other answered prayers that provided more faith to my soul than I thought possible.

But in the midst of all this, I had wavered. I had doubts. Nothing in that season seemed to be working out. Even the job my husband landed looked like it was lost for a while. The extra money we brought in barely paid the bills and put food on the table. Our funds were all depleted again.

I was teetering on the edge of despair.

But even though the church's aide money was gone and my husband's job was again at risk, I went to church and continued praying. I didn't want to feel the despair anymore. I was upset about things, and I didn't like it. I could see that my relationship with Jesus was sliding away a little bit, into a place where I put the blame on Him instead of the trust He deserved.

As I sang in worship, my chains of sorrow, doubt, and guilt slid away and my heart soared. I was again convinced that nothing is too big for God. As this realization struck, I felt completely different. Joy crept back into my soul. I had come out of pain into a place of comfort. In Matthew 11:28-30, (NIV), Jesus tells us,

> Come to me, all you who are weary and burdened, and I will give you rest. Take my yoke upon you and learn from me, for I am gentle and humble in heart, and you will find rest for your souls. For my yoke is easy and my burden is light.

This is one of those verses I'd always wondered about. I'd somehow gotten the notion that Christianity meant that pain was good. Our culture teaches us that it is a faith that makes us deny ourselves of anything good or pleasing.

That is just not true. God is our Father. He wants good things for us, even when our sin gets in the way, just like we want the best for our children even when they are willfully misbehaving. My yoke is one of sin, doubt, shame, and despair. My yoke is the burden of unbelieving. My yoke is my lack of trust in an all-powerful God of the universe who loves me as His own child.

Jesus wants us to drop that yoke. He wants you to trust He can do all that *and* much more than we can ever ask, more than you even have the courage to ask.

God doesn't always answer in the way you want. This particular time, His good purpose aligned with my more selfish desires. (Although asking for provision for my family is not totally selfish, in this case, there was a selfish element.) But often it's not like that. He may have a plan that involves allowing you to lose something you hold dear. While I learned to trust that God would provide, there was no way for me to know if He wanted me to keep my home or if our destiny would lie in another town, state, or even country.

And the thing is, I can't worry about that. His will, His plan, and His purpose is always best, even if I'd rather stay right where I am.

That day in church, I put down my worry and embraced His will. Homelessness, relying on the kindness of others, losing everything, and relocating were all painful options to me, but I was willing to accept His perfect will because I knew it was better than my selfish desires.

Place your despair at the foot of Jesus' cross. He can ease your pain from you, but you must give it to Him first. This means unloading your heart of every last bit. And if you need to wake up tomorrow and do it again, do it. Our God is patient and loving and understands that it takes a long time for His children to fully surrender.

Then buckle up for the heart-changing journey ahead.

Chapter 7

Dealing with Sin in Your Heart:
Fear and Anxiety

For God has not given us a spirit of fear, but of power and of love and of a sound mind. Therefore do not be ashamed of the testimony of our Lord, nor of me His prisoner, but share with me in the sufferings for the gospel according to the power of God, who has saved us and called us with a holy calling, not according to our works, but according to His own purpose and grace which was given to us in Christ Jesus before time began, but has now been revealed by the appearing of our Savior Jesus Christ, who has abolished death and brought life and immortality to light through the gospel. — 2 Timothy 1:7-10, NKJV

When you are raising a child with special needs, there is troubling uncertainty about today and your child's future. Kids on the spectrum seem to have a long checklist of issues—behavioral, physical, medical, social, emotional—and we feel like we only have two hands to deal with them all. "Who will take care of my child when I'm gone?" is a question I've heard from almost everyone I've met raising an autistic child.

Who indeed?

The answer to that question, we know, deep down in our hearts, is the Lord. But between here and there, we must do what's right and do our best to protect them from harm. How can we trust the Lord with our fears while making the best choices for our kids? We need to rely on God's promises while listening for His guiding answers.

Countering Fear and Doubt with God's Promises

1 John 4:18 (ESV) says, "There is no fear in love, but perfect love casts out fear. For fear has to do with punishment, and whoever fears has not been perfected in love."

I struggled with this verse that so many people shared with me. I'm not perfect, so how can I combat fear? What does punishment have to do with it?

The meaning of this verse is less complicated than I first thought. After prayerful contemplation, I see it this way:

- Fear is a way we punish ourselves.
- If we place our trust in the Lord with one thing at a time, He can conquer our fears, one by one.

- As He moves us past our own anxiety, we grow to trust Him more and more and experience more of His perfect love.
- Meanwhile our love for Him is in the process of being perfected. We will never be perfect in this life, but each day, we become a little more Christ-like.

That's a lot! Let's break each one down.

Fear is a form of self-inflicted punishment.

I used to be afraid of everything. When my mother was pregnant with me, she was not yet saved. A friend brought her to a medium, who told her that her child would die. As a result, my mother was terrified that I would die. She was a helicopter parent before that phrase was coined.

This fear infected everything in my childhood. To this day, I cannot ride a bike or roller skate because I inherited her fears of me falling and getting seriously injured. I'm terrified of heights because my mother nervously hovered just riding the elevator in a tall building. I have a phobia of letting go of the edge of the pool so I cannot swim. Even as an adult, she told me never to go on a cruise (as she once did) because there were pirates and smugglers on the seas. To this day, I still struggle with driving because of fear.

All of this was done in love and even though she got saved, the fear never left her. I've struggled with fear my whole life. I feel that is now my responsibility, but I wish my mother hadn't responded this way.

The worst part is that this all started because of a lie from a psychic told her. My siblings and I all outlived my mom, who lived into her eighties. This is one of the reasons why God does not want you messing around with mediums and fortune-telling.

Satan planted a fear in my mother which was passed on to me. The difference is, I'm aware of it and the damage it's done in my life. In reality, fear is nothing more than a shackle that enslaves us. And when we are afraid, the enemy laughs because he knows it makes us powerless.

God can conquer all our fears.

I decided to take back my life back, but it isn't my own power I'm counting on. If I follow Jesus and do what He asks, He will empower me, a little more each day, to do what He calls me to do. Because I know He is faithful, I know that I can do whatever He wills no matter how challenging.

Trusting God has allowed to me to conquer scary situations. I learned to drive and can get my family where they need to be. I've been able to speak on stage and online, and I've been able to share my faith.

I've even conquered some fears completely. I used to be terrified of the dark. When we moved from New York City to the Poconos in Pennsylvania, the shift from urban living to a more rural life was shocking. My fear was amplified because my husband had a two-hour commute to his job, meaning he had to leave around 5:00AM. In the winter, this meant a long stretch alone in the dark for me. Having my daughter in January helped, but still those fears surrounded me.

As a result, I got up and did the only thing I knew wouldn't bring on any kind of fear: reading the Bible. I turned on the lights and got into the Word, all the while praying aloud for God to rebuke Satan, as I had seen my own mother do. I was, at this point, still on the fence about my salvation, but like I said, God's love is perfect. He cast that fear of the dark out of me. Within a year, my lifelong fear of the dark was completely gone.

I still have fears, but I have been calling out to the Lord to help me conquer them, one by one. The bigger and more deeply entrenched the fear, the harder it is to entrust it to the Lord. But I know that He is always faithful, and I know that even in this world, all my fears can disappear if I surrender them to Him. He will empower me to do whatever He wills even if it means conquering the biggest fears in my life.

God's love for us is perfect

We won't always admit it, but there may be times when we don't believe this. Even in our doubt, even when we don't think we're hearing from God, even when we think our prayers go unanswered, the great mystery of God is that His love is unchanging and unconditional. Once we are His, we are truly and completely loved, each and every day, no matter what we do.

In Romans, Paul teaches us:

> Very rarely will anyone die for a righteous person, though for a good person someone might possibly dare to die. But God demonstrates his own love for us in this: While we were still sinners, Christ died for us. Since we have now been justified by his blood, how much more shall we be saved from God's wrath through Him! For if, while we were God's enemies, we were reconciled to Him through the death of his Son, how much more, having been reconciled, shall we be saved through His life! — Romans 5:7-10, NIV

Imagine someone you don't like, someone who has consistently hurt you and turned his or her back and betrayed you. Do you have an actual person in mind? Can you see him or her?

Now imagine wanting to help that person so badly that you'd be willing to sacrifice your own child specifically in order to save him or her.

I can't think of any human I know who I would be certain could do this, no matter how long they've been a Christian. I know I couldn't.

Yet this is what our merciful God did for us. He pined for our presence in His heart so badly that He asked His son to make this sacrifice. And Jesus willingly said "yes" to this incomparable sacrifice, from His arrest to His dying breath.

Every moment that the choice was presented to Him, He offered Himself up to God's will for our salvation. At any moment, Jesus could have said, "That's enough. Father, send your angels to get Me out of this." Since He is king of the universe, they would have had to obey.

But He didn't. He stepped out of heaven and freely give His all in obedience to the Father through the entire ordeal of His trial and death. And though He asked the Father to take away this cup, He didn't even complain when God denied His request. But He did continue to speak the truth, even to the thief on the cross beside Him, to tell of the wonderful paradise that we sinners get to share because of His perfect, obedient love.

This is what the mighty God of Heaven has done for you.

Our love for Him is being perfected

As you walk along your journey with Jesus, God will grow your love for Him. One thing I have learned over the years is that He does not want us to stay where we are in our walk, but He wants us to develop into mature Christians. This is the only way we can grow into the people He has created us to be. He will make sure we grow, by putting us in the same situations over and over until we see the light. And we know that we grow the most in times of difficulty. As we do, our character becomes more Christ-like, and so does our love for Him.

When we are new Christians, we are amazed by how He loved us while we were still sinners. Jesus will, however, push you past that. I remember the day I saw clearly how completely unworthy I was. At the time, I'd been a Christian for about five years. God had called a small group of us out of our church because the leaders were not listening to God's direction. The Holy Spirit brought us together, and we started meeting together every Sunday morning in the home of one of our leaders. I attended this home church for several years.

One of the early studies we did was about how we were created as a gift from God, the Father, to the Son. That study completely amazed me and showed me how completely worthless and broken I was outside of the Father's love. And yet, somehow, some way, He still chose *me*.

I can't explain why He chose me. I haven't got a clue. I'm the girl who got picked last in gym all the time. I was never popular. I know how to write well, but that's it. I'm not beautiful, athletic, or extra generous. I can be a real jerk if I'm not careful. I have a temper that I've learned how to hide most of the time and a huge ego.

One of my biggest faults that God healed was playing the victim—so embarrassing, everyone hates a fake victim! Worse yet, I had no idea I was even doing that. I'm selfish. I have yelled and sometimes even cursed in front of my kids.

Before I was saved, I rejected and waffled about Christianity because I was too selfish. I didn't want to give up my definition of myself. I was afraid to have a shift in my politics. I refused to let go of the sinful things that brought me pleasure. I was prideful and egotistical, and I worshipped at the altar of myself and the altar of logic.

Yet, God did not reject me for any of those reasons. He has gently, considerately, and in ways I never expected pulled me away from all those sins. A few times, He has had to take a heavy-handed approach, where the discipline hurt so bad, I felt like dying. That's been rare, but God only uses it when I'm intentionally blinding myself to correcting my choices. The upside to this kind of discipline, though, is that it completely eradicates your desire for this sin.

Mostly, the Lord has gently guided me past my own incorrect opinions and preferences by showing me His truth. Before too long, I was no longer attached to a particular belief, thought, or frame of mind that came from anywhere outside of God.

The Lord showed me that He already knew all those things about me. He had a better plan for me, one that would make me a better person, one that even I could love: a more devoted parent, a more forgiving wife, a more trusted friend, and a faithful servant. His perfect love cast out my fear of not being the "great" person I mistakenly thought I was.

When I let Him undo me, I started to become the person He wanted me to be, and I discovered that was the real me! It's been a blessing and an honor to be a daughter of the King.

Regret: Wishing for Things Past

Sometimes, we get caught up in wishing that things now were like they used to be. Remember when school was easy and joyful for our children? Remember before your child regressed into this issue or developed that behavior? Remember the time before head-banging, self-injury, meltdowns?

You might find yourself praying this: Why, God, can't you make it like it used to be?

But even in all these things, God has His purpose. If we turn to the amazing — and painful — stories of motherhood in the Bible, we can see that God wants you to move forward in Him rather than wishing for the past.

Let's take two Biblical moms who don't often get a lot of credit for teaching us truth: Lot's wife, whose role in the Bible is so small she isn't even named, and Eve, the mother of mankind. These women experienced hardship but took completely different approaches to them. Only one of them looked back, with disastrous results.

Lot's Wife: Frozen and Crumbling

This scripture introduces Lot and his family, who lived in a place called Sodom. (Read the full account in Genesis 19.) God chooses to destroy Sodom because its people are so wicked. I know that this is hard to think about today, but it was a city filled with all kinds of sins, including regular child sacrifice. I believe that not a single person there knew God and that most of them worshipped an evil, false god.

It's horrible to think of those child sacrifices, but we must realize that in dying, those children probably went directly to God instead of growing up into evil people themselves. Since so many were sacrificed to fire, who knows how many were abused or molested or harmed in some other way during their short lives?

Before destroying the city, angels came to rescue Lot, the only Godly man in the region, and his family. The angel relocated them to another town, with the instruction not to look back. His wife gets just one line in the Bible:

But his wife looked back behind him, and she became a pillar of salt. – Genesis 19:26

It's hard to understand specifically why this happened, but I can venture a guess. In 2015, my husband found old videos of my older daughter, Amelia, when she was three years old. She has Down syndrome, and at the time I watched this video, she was twelve years old. In this video, she was amazing, just like any three-year-old: cute, adorable, verbal, and completely understandable. She was engaged, focused, and active. You would never know she had a disability except for the physical features that indicated Down syndrome.

More than a decade later, she still has difficulties with her speech. She often talks in third person about herself, scripts her language from movies, and uses correlation to describe certain things. Often, she mumbles and is hard to understand. Although her challenges are improving, watching that video was heartbreaking. How did this happen? How did she lose her speech in this way? When did her problems start?

Asking those questions has some merit, I grant you, but I see lots of moms stuck in a place they shouldn't be by looking back at what a child has lost. This is especially true for parents of kids with regressive autism. If an event that I cannot determine or prove truly stole my daughter's abilities, I have two choices:

- Look back in anger and regret and grumble over what was "stolen." Like Lot's wife, I can be frozen into a crumbling statue of salt, looking, blaming, arguing, and letting my heart fill with hate and desperation until I'm too lost to do anything without falling apart.
- Take Paul's advice of "forgetting those things which are behind and reaching forward to those things which are ahead." (Phil 3:13b) Paul is encouraging us by sharing his example of moving forward into the things God has designed for us to live His purpose.

Are there times when you need to dig up the past? Yes, sometimes when needed, for example discovering the starting point of a condition. But you must avoid getting stuck there. It was worth it, for example, for me to dig down to find out what exactly happened to cause Amelia to lose her speech skills so that I could address that issue. Reflecting on the past to solve a problem is not a bad thing. That's especially true if it's a problem of the heart. But medical history can be a key step for helping our children too.

However, when you get stuck in the past, it is hard to hear the wisdom of God, who is telling you to move forward with your life. If you can't separate the past from your present, you cannot help your child no matter how "right" you think you are.

Let's take a look at another Biblical mother and how she moved past failure.

Eve: Moving Forward in Spite of Sin

We meet Eve in Genesis 2 through 4. She was created as a "helpmate" to Adam, the first man. While in the Garden of Eden, Satan appeared to her in the form of a serpent and tempted her to break the only rule God made for the first two humans: not to eat from the tree of knowledge of good and evil.

Wow, Eve, that's a big screw up. (Let's not forget that Adam was supposed to protect her. Shouldn't he have at least said, "No! Stop!"?) Later, when God confronted them with their disobedience, He curses them both. This is what God said to Eve:

"I will greatly multiply your sorrow and your conception;
In pain you shall bring forth children;
Your desire shall be for your husband,
And he shall rule over you." —Genesis 3:16, NKJV

Yikes. I know if it were ME, I'd be like, "Hey Adam, I am SOOOO outta here. We had fun and all, but sorry—sorrow and pain? No way I'm having babies. Later." But Eve? She stuck it out. She knew the curse and still she had babies with Adam—at least three sons and at least one daughter. Of course, we know the story doesn't seem to end well because her firstborn son would kill her second.

It's time to return to the story of Cain and Abel. There is a temptation here to credit Adam and Eve with being bad parents, but something we need to remember is that Abel was a good kid—a *really* good kid. Abel was a shepherd and knew to give God the best offering and the fat of his finest sheep to please God.

Now, in the Garden of Eden, God walked with Adam and Eve. But once they were cast out, He no longer was by their side, helping and advising people. So how did Abel know to give the best offering to God?

There's only one way he could have known: Mom and Dad taught him well. In fact, Abel was so devoted to God during his short life that he is mentioned in Hebrews 11:4, NIV also known as "Faith's Hall of Fame:"

By faith Abel brought God a better offering than Cain did. By faith he was commended as righteous when God spoke well of his offerings. And by faith Abel still speaks, even though he is dead.

You are never going to convince me that Adam and Eve did not spend a good amount of time teaching their children about God. After all, they got kicked out of Heaven! What a painful lesson. And don't we, as parents, work hard to make sure our kids don't repeat our mistakes? I cringe when I see Zoe or Amelia display unpleasant behaviors that I've displayed in front of them! But I also work hard to share good Godly habits, like reading the gospel to them, praying at night, apologizing for anything wrong I've done in front of them, and so on. I'm confident that

Adam and Eve taught their children about the Almighty God and Abel took those lessons to heart.

But just like life today, a child raised properly can take an unrighteous path. As we already discussed, their other son, Cain, a farmer, gave God a gift too, but it wasn't the best he had to offer. All we know is what God sees: "He did not respect Cain and his offering." One sin leads to another until he murders his brother.

While there are things we can blame on parents, we need to look at the full story. Given human nature, it's natural that Adam and Eve would have a son who grew up to be the second sinner, but they *also* raised a son who grew up to be the first person in Heaven. I like to think that Eve, with sorrow in her heart for the mistake she could never take back, set her children on her knee and told them *exactly* what it had been like to walk in the presence of God.

Can't you just imagine Abel's eyes light up as a child? And Cain? Well, maybe he was bored or distracted or not paying attention. "Oh Mom's at it again with *that* story." I know I can relate to having two children who have completely different reactions, tastes, and likes to just about everything!

The reaction of Eve's sons was likely different and that too was God's plan. With perfect grace, the Lord chose Abel who would be first in heaven and famous forever, even without ever having any descendant. But murder, anger, and jealously lurked in Cain's heart, and Abel demonstrated love for God by giving Him his finest. Surely, he learned that from his parents, in some small way.

Eve has this to look back on: committing the first sin of all time and raising a son who is the first murderer, of her other child. Wouldn't you be completely done with childbearing at this point? But, she also raised a child who pleased the Lord! She went on to have a third child, Seth. We see that Eve is not only the first sinner among humans, but also a woman who could move beyond the horrid mistakes of her past to live out her duty as a wife and mother.

Even if the past looks brighter, we don't have time machines to return there. We have come down the path that God has required of us, and we must move forward. We must let go of our expectation of what our child "should" have been by worldly standards. Like Eve, we can't determine our future results. And while we will make mistakes, we can still move forward to better lives for our kids every day. That's how I feel about Amelia and Zoe. I will never give up guiding them, even as they are adults.

We must move forward for our children and for our purpose in this world, just like Eve did.

And thank God she did! From that precious line of the third son came our own blessed Redeemer, Jesus Christ. Imagine if she had gotten stuck in the past? There'd be a world, but no people to fill it, no me and you, and none of our beautiful children who fill our hearts and minds with beauty, sorrow, pain, and love.

There'd be no Savior to make all our suffering worth the eternal life that awaits us at the end. And that's a thing I would not trade for any perfect world.

Chapter 8

Finding the Support You Need

Now the multitude of those who believed were of one heart and one soul; neither did anyone say that any of the things he possessed was his own, but they had all things in common. And with great power the apostles gave witness to the resurrection of the Lord Jesus. And great grace was upon them all. Nor was there anyone among them who lacked; for all who were possessors of lands or houses sold them, and brought the proceeds of the things that were sold, and laid them at the apostles' feet; and they distributed to each as anyone had need.
— Acts 4:32-35, NKJV

If you've ever been part of a close-knit, caring, serving church, then you may have had the blessing and privilege of the kind of support the early church had, as described here in Acts. They all took care of each other.

While this shows how well Jesus' first disciples provided for each other's physical and financial needs, I'm sure they also provided help for emotional needs and support for families, like sharing childcare especially if anyone became injured or imprisoned or was required to travel to spread the gospel. And you know they had to have helped each other when they or one of their children became sick or disabled.

Doesn't it sound wonderful?

Unfortunately, today's world is not as community based as it once was. Where once upon a time, your entire extended family would live down the block, nowadays you are lucky to live within driving distance of one or two relatives. We've substituted technology for distance, figuring it's okay to video chat with a loved one, until we realize that we've lost the joy that comes from physical contact or looking someone in the eye.

Covid-19 only escalated this separation. People became afraid to be around one another, and one by one, programs that help disabled children dried up or disappeared. Churches were no exception. Unfortunately, even before the pandemic, you'd be hard-pressed to find churches that supported older teen or adults with special needs. Some won't even provide care for young children with challenges, despite the fact that this population is growing.

If you have a child on the autism spectrum, you know that physical distance is not the only barrier in your life. Your friends won't always journey with you because they don't understand the realities of raising a child on the autism spectrum. Your family may roll their eyes at you. You may not have a giving church, or you might have no church at all.

You need support.

Why Every Parent Raising an Autistic Child Needs Support

First, I want to be clear that you are not alone. Jesus is with you this entire journey. You are the perfect parent for your child, and that means the challenges that you face serve God's purpose for you. This is difficult to accept, but it is true. No trial can come before you that God did not approve.

But trials are difficult. It is true that with the Holy Spirit and the Word of God, we can face and overcome anything. However, without the support of people who have walked in your shoes, you may struggle.

By support, I specifically mean that you need to connect with other moms or parents who also have children with an autism diagnosis. Parents of children who have no experience with autism don't understand what is involved in raising your child or the unique challenges he or she deals with, such as sensory issues, self-injury, or regression.

But if you know other autism families, there is nothing like that good friend who has been there, done that, and can throw an arm around your shoulder — even if it's a virtual one. Things may happen that you are unsure of — a behavior your child is showing, a reaction you feel that you don't think is Godly. Befriending other parents who have walked in your shoes helps you maintain your sanity as you discover common ground.

Some time ago, I helped a lady at my church move. Despite the fact that she was a single mom to an adult son with severe autism and I was a married woman with an eleven-year-old autistic daughter, we had a wonderful conversation. We connected on so many things! Yes, every person on the autism spectrum is completely unique, and yet our vastly different children had similarities that instantly built a bond between us. Although she moved away shortly after, it taught me a lot about the importance of communicating with other parents.

And she is just one of many other parents raising kids on the spectrum who I count as friends. In short, befriending other autism parents will show you that you are not alone!

The Importance of Prayer in Finding Community

This should actually be your first step: to pray that the Lord provides you with friends and support for your family. I cannot tell you how often the Lord has answered my prayers for support and friends. Most of the time, these didn't happen overnight. Sometimes the friends I met went away, but it was always to make room for the people He wants in my life for a new season.

When you are praying, be specific in asking the Lord for your needs. If you want a friend who understands what you are going through, ask God to put a Godly woman in your life who is raising a child on the spectrum.

Consider what else you need in a relationship, information, help, guidance, a prayer partner? Ask the Lord specifically for your needs and your community.

Keep in mind that God's choice may not look like what you expected. When I attended Bible study, God put an older woman in my path. I followed her guidance on many spiritual matters for years, before learning that she too had raised a child on the spectrum. He had passed away years before I met her, but she has been a great source of advice and comfort.

That doesn't mean those are the only people you'll ever meet, but it does mean you'll need to put yourself out there. You can't meet other parents by staying home all the time. You need to get out of your home, with and without your children. Attend a Bible study, bring your child to activities designed for disabled children, participate in walks and other fundraising activities, etc. You don't necessarily need to volunteer, but you do need to be out and about so others can find you.

As you do this, pray for great discernment and wisdom. Don't force-fit a relationship that you suspect God has not put into your life. Even good, Christian relationships can be against God's will, depending on the timing and the situation. For example, if you've made friends with people your husband can't stand, that can harm your marriage. (This is true whether or not your husband is a believer.)

What's most important is that the relationships that you build support you and your relationship with the Lord and your child. Opposing God's wishes in this area will bring you pain and attachments that are costly to your soul. Those relationships can easily lead to hurt and regret.

Let's talk a bit more about regret because it's something every parent has — particularly those of us raising children on the autism spectrum.

Letting Go of Regret

I have never met a mom of a child with special needs who didn't second-guess some decision or other she made or maybe even *all* of her decisions. The fact is, as a parent you have to make difficult choices with the information you have at the time. If you know differently later, then that little chorus of self-doubt mumbles in your ear that you've failed because you made the best choice at the time with what you knew back then. Maybe it's best to tell you right now: that little voice could be yours OR it may be Satan.

It's certainly not the voice of the Lord if it's filling you with guilt and regret over things you did not know.

One of the reasons you need to find support is to remind yourself that you are not alone. The choices and challenges of raising a child on the autism spectrum can be complex, but there may be someone in your community who has been through what you're experiencing. She can give you the advice you need or show you a solution you hadn't thought of before.

The right support system can provide you with confidence to move forward with the choices you make. This type of support can loosen the hold that the enemy's tool of regret has on your life.

Types of Support Systems You Might Need

With all that being said, here are a few different types of support systems that can provide you with the help you need to raise your child. Continue to ask God for wisdom, guidance, and discernment in deciding which ones you need most and where you can find them.

- **A partner in arms:** Hopefully, you have a spouse or a coparent to support you, but if not, you'll need someone who has your back. This can be a friend, mentor, or close family member — anyone who is ready to accept you and your child as you are right now.
- **A good practitioner:** This can be a medical doctor, D.O., homeopath, naturopath, doctor who specializes in therapies and protocols for autism, nutritionist, chiropractor, etc. You do need to be careful with treatments and therapies to make sure they are not ungodly. My recommendation is to find a doctor who is knowledgeable about functional nutrition since many are not, and nutrition is often key to solving behavior and physical issues in children on the autism spectrum. You may also need someone experienced in alternative therapies for autism, such as a naturopath or an M.D./D.O. (Autism conferences are a great resource to find these practitioners.) Keep in mind that these providers do not always have to be local, as many practitioners now work virtually.
- **Another mom raising a kid with autism:** You cannot friend too many of these. Moms like us come from all ages, socio-economic backgrounds, faiths, and cultures. You can get a great perspective on how to help your child and, of course, a companion who understands your family's unique challenge.
  Find someone you can have a laugh with, or just forget about the kiddos for a bit. Parenting a child with autism is a 24/7 gig, with childcare providers being few and far between. However, if you can find someone who helps you smile even during difficult times, this is a blessing. Having someone who you can relate to and have fun with is part of self-care, too, and is important to keep you mentally healthy.
- **An advocate for education-related services:** These are people who work for *you*, not the school system. You can use a special education advocate, disability lawyer, supports coordinator, case worker, inclusion expert, wraparound service provider, etc. — and not necessarily at the same time. You may need help dealing with IEPs, 504 plans, difficult teachers, inclusion, problematic paraprofessionals, etc. Don't leave yourself short in this area but try to get an expert's advice.
  A word of caution here. Even the best advocates may be politically motivated, especially when it comes to funding for the services. I advise you to keep an appropriate business-only boundary when working with support providers.

- **Organizations that help with autism:** Some of my favorite support programs include National Autism Association, TACANow, local groups (ARC), and WrightsLaw.com, which provides advice about the laws governing disability services in the U.S. You can find out about many organizations at your local autism conferences as well.
- **Someone you can talk to about grown-up stuff:** You're a mom, but that's not the sum total of all you are. It's nice to get together with friends who have no kids or simply have something in common with you: faith, politics, a love of movies, etc. It's good to have friends to talk about interests that *don't* include your child—friends outside your autism mom tribe. I love my Facebook groups and my friends at the gym.
- **Professional help:** You may need a therapist or counselor for yourself, not just your child. I recommend you find a Christian counselor. Always screen them to make sure they practice with Biblically sound professionalism and are a good fit for you.
- **Your own healthcare providers:** Your child needs you to be healthy and fit. Therapists, life coaches, fitness trainers, and your own health care professionals are a few examples. Be sure to take care of your own health as well.

Where to Find Support

Over the years, I have found support and friends going through similar struggles through different outlets. Many of the people I met were also desperate for connection as it can be difficult to come by. For example, many families raising kids on the spectrum spend major holidays alone.

Find others who face the same trials, challenges, and successes. You can share resources and critical information on who to trust and who to avoid.

Where can you go to find people and parents who have been through the same thing and can help you build your community? While I wish there could always be "in real life" scenarios, sometimes you'll have to find community virtually.

Some places you can go to find other parents raiding kids on the spectrum include:

- Facebook groups
- National Autism Association (NAA), an organization that helps parents of kids on the spectrum connect and share advice
- A local chapter of TACANow, which provides both local and virtual support
- Local special needs and autism events
- ARC or ARCH services
- Your local autism organizations
- Churches that provide respite care or special needs care during services

- State or county sponsored respite care services
- Activities for families with special needs or autism
- Support groups for families with autism

Another place to connect with other families raising a child on the spectrum is at autism conferences. The NAA's National Autism Conference and other outlets have some great national and local events, where parents and caregivers can find a host of information and resources to help their children and train on prominent issues that affect them. It's not just a place to share information. These events can help you find and connect with your tribe so you can build relationships with other families. This, too, can help your kids connect with other autistic children and begin to build friendships.

With autism prevalence numbers consistently on the rise, the number of support organizations and providers is also rising. You should be able to find the help you need locally and online; you only need to look. Be sure to do so with God's guidance.

Chapter 9

Dealing with Friends and Family

Bear with each other and forgive one another if any of you has a grievance against someone. Forgive as the Lord forgave you. – Colossians 3:13, NIV

We've all been through it. Someone we care about has hurt us, betrayed us, or dumped us that we think is because of our child. Maybe they accused our child of something he or she didn't do. Maybe they accused us of being bad parents because our kids struggle to behave. Maybe they said or did something unthinkable, like using a nasty word or "forgetting" to invite us somewhere.

For all that autism advocates have done over the years to educate people on this topic, you'll still run into people who don't "get" it—even among your own friends and family. There's so much they don't understand about why your child does or says the things he does; why she's too loud, why he's not potty trained yet, why she hits people. *You* know it's not bad behavior but a coping device or a health issue, but it can be hard to convince people who don't live with the day-in-day-out complexities of autism.

It hurts when those are the people closest to you. It's happened to us several times. The pee incident. The candle incident. The time I couldn't go to a wedding because I couldn't travel that far with my child, which insulted a family member. The time my kid made the egregious error of touching all the food on the plate but only eating one piece.

The worst part is that when the criticism comes from people you love, you end up feeling guilty, as if the situation is your fault: my fault for attending the event, my fault for not yet healing my child's issues, my fault for living too far to host the holiday myself. I cringed with guilt when my child did things that were the result of her disability.

I don't cringe anymore. The fact is, my daughter is a child of God, and I am working hard to teach her about the Lord, heal her health, improve her behaviors, and making the best decisions I can all around.

I am doing my best, and I have the Holy Spirit to convict me when I'm not. Everything else is false guilt, and that only comes from one source: Satan.

Dealing with False Guilt

Before we start to handle the situation, we need to take care of any false guilt we may be carrying. We cannot deal with our relationships if we are walking around with false impressions of ourselves. So how do we manage it?

First, make sure that your guilt is false. Is there anything you knowingly left out when planning for your child to spend time with friends and family due to selfishness, laziness, or some other quality that was on you? I'm talking intentional errors that have a root of something sinful, like spite, not run-of-the-mill busyness, or forgetfulness. It may be there was a step you neglected, so ask the Holy Spirit to reveal anything that you may have not done on purpose that could have made the situation better. It could be something as simple as praying about the situation beforehand.

I caution you, though, not to hang onto this for a long time. Pray and then be done with it. The Spirit will reveal any shortcomings you need to know but it is likely that you took all the care you could in making sure this visit would be uneventful.

The reality is our children display new and unexpected behaviors when they are in unfamiliar or stressful situations. They are also incredibly curious about new surroundings and may explore this new environment in ways your host might not find acceptable. And of course, behaviors may be triggered by something that they don't like or understand or that scares them.

If you did what you could and you have been helping your child as best you can, any guilt you feel is false. Remember what Romans 8:1 says: There is therefore now no condemnation for those who are in Christ Jesus. Unfortunately, it is true that people may condemn you for the actions of your child, when in fact, they shouldn't be condemning anyone at all. Those can come from your Christian brothers and sisters, or unbelievers.

Here's the thing, though: Jesus sees it all. He sees the work you've put into your child and the work you've put into planning for your child to see friends and family and attend events. He also sees the times you've missed holidays, vacations, and outings because you were certain your child could not handle it. He is there, right beside you, even when you are sad that others don't know or see the beauty in your son or daughter. He loves you, and He will never condemn you — or your child — for behaviors that have not or cannot be addressed.

On that, you can rely. Discard any feelings of unwarranted guilt, confess any true guilt, and move on with doing the best you can for your child.

Dealing with Your Family

Once you've dealt with guilt, you can now address what to do when you want your child to have a relationship with your loved ones who simply don't understand. There are no easy answers for this, but there are steps you can take to build bridges without losing your cool:

1. Forgive them.
2. Educate them.
3. Pray for them.
4. Set boundaries.
5. Show them love.

Forgiving Those who Hurt You or Your Child

Whether or not they are a believer, Jesus commands us to forgive one another "7 times 70 times" (Matthew 18:22). That actually means to forgive someone as often as they sin against us, not just 490 times. In other words, don't keep score!

If you have previously had a good relationship with a person, the situation may be more painful than others. That will be the most challenging person to forgive, but you can do it with the help of the Holy Spirit. Remember that forgiveness is really between you and the Lord. In Matthew 6:14-15 (NKJV), Jesus tells his disciples:

> For if you forgive men their trespasses, your heavenly Father will also forgive you. But if you do not forgive men their trespasses, neither will your Father forgive your trespasses.

This is right after Jesus teaches His disciples the Lord's Prayer. I was taught this prayer by rote as a child. How many times did I say it, before and after my salvation, not realizing what was meant by this line:

> "And forgive us our trespasses as we forgive those who trespass against us." — Matthew 6:12, NKJV

Jesus does forgive us unconditionally, so this line does not mean that we need to forgive others to obtain forgiveness ourselves. What it means is that we are pledging to forgive others "as" or like the Lord forgave us.

In Colossians, Paul tells us this:

> "...Bearing with one another and, if one has a complaint against another, forgiving each other; as the Lord has forgiven you, so you also must forgive. — Colossians. 3:13, ESV

Forgiving others, then, is not an option. It's a commandment, and we are to forgive just exactly as God forgave us.

That's not easy. How many of us have wished to rain down coals on the heads of our family, or others who have hurt us and our children, played us for fools or made a mockery of their care?

And what if the person is not sorry? We must remember that the Lord forgave us while we were still sinners. Therefore, we are to forgive others even if they have not acknowledged or even understood that they did anything wrong.

No, this is not easy. It may take everything you have. After all, most parents who love their children work on the principle of "hurt me and I can deal with it, but hurt my kid and I will hurt you back."

That is not God's way. As children of the Almighty Father, we are called to be forgiving. We need to continually hand our hurt over to the Lord. If you stay mired in pity, anger, loathing, or grudges, you are opening the door to Satan. All he needs is a foothold to detract you from your duty as a mother and start you down the path of sin and destruction.

Withholding forgiveness, though, doesn't just open the door for sin. It can harm your own health and well-being. Today, scientific research demonstrates that negative thoughts and feelings can impact both physical and mental health. These thoughts lead to or exasperate illness and other medical conditions. They can also lead to depression, anxiety, rage, and other psychological issues.

So how do we forgive? It's not going to be easy, but it can be accomplished if we take things one step at a time. Here are some ways you can begin your journey to forgiveness:

- Remember all the good things about your relationship from the past. Create a gratitude list of those things and thank God for them.
- Get past the small slights. If it's something that isn't harmful or life-changing to your family, consider letting it go.
- Remember they have never walked in your shoes. It's possible they never will. All of that is in God's hands. And never having raised your child, they cannot know all the intricacies of your precious child or even the basic challenges of raising a child on the spectrum.
- Pray for them in a positive way. Most people pray the person will change to their liking. Instead, I encourage you to pray for their salvation and for God to bless them. This will help to soften your heart toward them.
- Set boundaries that protect you and your child. This may involve avoiding events, at least temporarily, or not engaging in arguments or even discussions about your child.
- Know when to walk away. The sad fact is that sometimes people cannot accept the reality of this situation and will continually blame you. I wouldn't do this lightly, but ask the Lord to confirm if a bit of space and distance — at least temporarily — is the right thing to do. It may be better to pray for their salvation and well-being from a distance, than to be constantly confronted and tempted to sin with an angry or hurtful reaction.

Forgiveness is necessary for you to move forward. Forgiveness helps you to be a good parent and combat self-pity that can lead to "victimhood." On the other hand, an unforgiving heart will lead to bitterness, and that is a destructive force in our lives. Ephesians 4:31-33 (NIV) says:

Get rid of all bitterness, rage and anger, brawling and slander, along with every form of malice. Be kind and compassionate to one another, forgiving each other, just as in Christ God forgave you.

I like that this verse goes right from all those feelings God wants you to remove from your heart, including bitterness, and then goes directly to forgiveness! This verse teaches us how to act toward other people: be kind, compassionate, and forgiving.

This might take a while, and that's okay. Remember that this is a process. As you move through it, continually ask God for guidance and healing in your family. Families like ours need all the support we can get. We do not need to deal with the added stress of complex relationships so you may need to choose between moving forward with the relationship or ending it. Before you do, though, be sure that the Lord is guiding you on how to handle your loved ones.

Educate What You Can When It's Appropriate

If you are moving forward with your relationship, your next course of action is to educate your family member or friend as best you can on why your child has these struggles. This will only happen if they are willing to listen, which is why forgiveness is the first piece of communicating with your family. Most of us understand why our child cannot help reacting a certain way, even if we don't have a way to improve the behavior.

You may balk at this idea, but keep in mind that this is *not* about making excuses for your child. Even a child with a severe disability can misbehave. As parents, we often can discern a rebellious action versus a reaction caused by our child's behavioral or social challenges. Those around us, however, don't always understand that there's a difference. In this case, you are explaining the real physical, mental, and emotional consequences that occur in your child as a result of autism or related issues. Keep your explanation factual but simple.

It's worth noting that your explanation might not sink in at the time. One year, we had to miss a family wedding for a close relative. Unbeknownst to my family, this was a difficult decision for me because I love to see my family, and I love weddings! Unfortunately, it just was too complex to figure out who could take care of our daughters, how we could get there, how to afford the airfare, etc. I tried my best, but the logistics failed me. The bride was upset and angry. I don't blame her! And I was touched that our presence mattered.

However, the people in question eventually came to understand our situation and forgave us. You might be thinking, *Why should they forgive you? You did nothing wrong!*

The fact is that none of that matters. What matters is your Christ-like attitude. Is it really so bad to be forgiven when you haven't done anything wrong? Is your offense more important than bringing peace to the situation? Jesus hung on the cross without ever having done a single thing wrong in His life. So yes, you can take the blame if it brings peace to your family. And please, before you consider turning your back on your family, remember that action could have lifelong repercussions on you and your children. If I could turn back time and revisit how I handled other family situations, I would do it in a heartbeat. The truth is, I regret the loss of those relationships, even if I was challenged on how to save them. Don't make this mistake if you don't have to!

Jesus preached "turning the other cheek" even after someone slaps you. While we can spend a long time examining and unearthing this verse from Matthew 5:39, we need to remember that it's talking about treatment from someone evil. Surely your relatives aren't evil, although they may be unsaved. However, they are sinners, whether or not they are saved.

Instead, I prefer to consider Luke 6:31:

Do to others as you would have them do to you.

If this is a struggle, you may want to reflect on your own past treatment of others. Before you had a child with a diagnosis of autism, did you ever pass judgment on unruly children who you saw? Did you ever blame a parent when you saw a child acting up? Was there any time in your life you passed judgment on people you didn't know?

Only God can change the hearts and minds of those you love, and only you can choose not to be offended. Choose the high road because it is the Lord's very best for you.

Pray for Them

The best thing you can do for the people who oppose you is pray for them.

This is no easy task. Satan doesn't want you to pray for the family members who don't understand you, but God does. The Bible has a lot to say about prayer and its power:

- God commands us to pray for *all* things: *Do not be anxious about anything, but **in every situation**, by prayer and petition, with thanksgiving, present your requests to God. – Philippians 4:6, NIV*
- We are commanded to pray for each other, and such prayer can change things. *Therefore confess your sins to each other and **pray for each other** so that you may be healed. The prayer of a righteous person is **powerful and effective**. – James 5:16, NIV*
- We should pray confidently in faith that God has this issue in hand. *When I cry out to You, Then my enemies will turn back; This I know, because **God is for me**. – Psalm 56:9, NKJV*
- Pray for those that persecute you. *But I say to you, love your enemies, bless those who curse you, do good to those who hate you, and **pray for those who spitefully use you and persecute you**. – Matthew 5:44, NKJV*
- Jesus hears and answers our prayers, even if we don't like the answer: *And I will do whatever you ask in My Name, so that the Father may be glorified in the Son. **You may ask Me for anything in My Name, and I will do it**. – John 14:13-14 (NIV)*

- *Call on Me in the day of trouble*; I will deliver you, *and you will honor Me. – Psalm 50:15, NIV*

Yes, He will deliver you but you must honor Him. It's important to remember that prayer is a conversation with Jesus. There are no "wrong" prayers, but just like any loved one, we must be respectful to the Lord when we speak to Him. By this I mean sharing honestly and treating Him nicely. Yes, you can vent to the Lord but do not treat Him worse than you would treat your dearest friend, but open and honest.

While God's Word serves many purposes, we can always trust it to tell us how to manage even the most challenging situations. You should pray for all things, in all situations: the good, the bad, and the uncomfortable. The Bible does not tell us to pray for some things, but all things. Trust in the Lord and His Word. Be thankful, confess, praise, ask, and just generally talk to your friend Jesus throughout the course of your day. Pray confidently in God's power, even for those who persecute you. And remember to glorify God when He answers you.

If you are a child of God, the Lord hears and answers all your prayers, even about strained relationships. It may not be the answer we want or in the time we think we need it, but we must be confident.

Sometimes the solution will call for distance from your family. Sometimes it will challenge you to get closer to people who don't understand you. But always it will be for His glory.

You should, however, schedule time for prayer, scripture reading, and quiet time. This will help you more clearly hear His response to your request. You might even want to consider fasting. While you are waiting, you can always take steps to protect your heart in your relationship.

Setting Boundaries for Your Family

You may need to create and set boundaries for how and when you visit or interact with family. These can include any number of things, but here are a few that have worked in my family:

- Do a live video chat for an event that you cannot attend.
- Bring specialty food items for your child if he or she has allergies or is on a restricted diet.
- Visit for a limited amount of time so you do not upset your child. At a wedding, for example, you may want to attend either a wedding ceremony or the reception because the entire event might be too long for your child.
- Ask if there is a quiet area you can use as a retreat for your child to calm down when you arrive or at other times. My kids often enjoyed playing with other kids' toys, so let your host know things like these. Together, find a solution that will keep your child happy, such as bringing similar toys for your child.
- Ask if "no go" areas can be locked off. If not, you may want to avoid attending.
- If your child has certain triggers or behaviors (strobe lights, silly string, breaking small objects), or foods that he or she cannot eat, ask your host if there will be any that are accessible to your child and if there's a way to avoid that. If not, you have a reason for not attending.

This is just a sample of what you can ask or do. Talk to your family and friends to find ways to negotiate this barrier before it becomes a problem too big to resolve.

You need to communicate, too. One year, a beloved relative and I had a big family dispute for several months. One day, we decided to sit down face to face as our phone calls had not alleviated the issue.

It turned out that the entire problem was over one mistaken word. *One word!* Before you feel offended and break a relationship, really listen to what is being said. Repeat it back, as well, to confirm. Meet in person to discuss if possible or do a live video chat. Make sure they heard you and you heard them. Always give them the benefit of the doubt.

Show Your Love

A discussion like this might resolve the issue quickly — or not. It might reveal a bigger issue than a simple miscommunication. They might honestly think you are not doing your duty as a mom. Even if there is a mistake, too much might have been said or done to make things right.

In this case, your duty is simply to follow God's will. And His will is that you love the person who hurt you. How can you show them love? In the same ways you show everyone else:

- Try small acts of kindness, like cards and small gifts for no reason. You want them to know you are thinking of them.
- Offer an upfront apology — a sincere one — about the situation and your respect for their position.
- Tell them you miss them and show that you care about them by asking how they are doing.
- Request talking things out as time goes by.
- Continue to pray for them. If they are receptive to prayer, make sure they know you are.

By showing your love, you can help soften their hearts. Hopefully, in time they will see you as caring and kind rather than upset and angry. Prayer can go a long way to changing their minds and building relationships.

However, it's important to note that this might *not* happen. Even when doing all that you do, others may not respond. You must leave it in God's hands. While He can bring reconciliation anywhere He chooses, this might be a relationship you'll need to pass on.

There is one relationship He does not want you to pass on: your spouse. Let's see what He can do to help your marriage.

Chapter 10

Fighting for Your Marriage

Therefore a man shall leave his father and mother and be joined to his wife, and they shall become one flesh. — Genesis 2:24, NKJV
Note: This chapter is for married women, so you can move on to Chapter 11 if you are single, divorced, or widowed. I encourage you to read it if, however, if you are separated or planning to marry.

You may have heard that there are exceptionally high divorce rates among parents raising children with special needs, especially autism. However, the currently available data does not support the alleged 80 percent divorce rate. How high is it? The research is all over the board, but putting statistics aside let's address this realistically: Raising a child on the autism spectrum is often an extreme stressor on your marriage.

Many things can pull you apart as you walk through therapies, protocols, and interventions for your child. Your spouse may not be on board with a particular therapy, may not understand the value of a special diet, or may want to take over and do everything himself. Financial burdens can be a problem. Being available for date nights, sex, and other kinds of intimacy may seem impossible. And the primary caretaker of the child can often struggle with fatigue, depression, overwhelm, or even post-traumatic stress disorder.

How can we have the healthy marital relationship we — and our kids — deserve?

Before we dive in, let's hear what the Bible says about marriage. Marriage is particularly important to God because He designed it to be an illustration of His covenant with His people:

> For the husband is the head of the wife even as Christ is the head of the church, His body, and is Himself its Savior. Now as the church submits to Christ, so also wives should submit in everything to their husbands.
> Husbands, love your wives, just as Christ also loved the church and gave Himself for her, that He might sanctify and cleanse her with the washing of water by the word, that He might present her to Himself a glorious church, not having spot or wrinkle or any such thing, but that she should be holy and without blemish. — Ephesians 5:23-27, ESV

I know you may be thinking that I just jumped right into the controversial "submit" scripture. Let's set aside the debate about wives submitting for a moment to focus on the analogy this verse illustrates. In the second sentence, we can clearly read that a wife is meant to submit to her husband as the church is meant to submit to God. Marriage, then, is an illustration of the foundational relationship between the church and the Lord.

Marriage as a metaphor for our relationship with Jesus works like this:

- The church is the bride/wife. She is to respect (and, of course, love) her husband, support him, and follow his leadership. She also is an equal partner, with plenty of input and the ability to make decisions too, but when decisions are split or they are critical to the family's direction or finances, the husband may need to lead. In the same way, the church, that is, those who love and are committed to Jesus, are to follow His leading.
- Jesus is the groom/husband. In the Bible, the husband is charged with keeping his wife safe and holy. He is supposed to love and sacrifice for the wife and follow God's leading. Jesus sacrificed for His "bride" by laying down His life. He guides the church, and we follow His leading. He is under the direction and guidance of His Father.
- God is the groom's father. He directs Jesus. In the Bible, Jesus clearly says that His arrest and death were the will of the Father. The date of Jesus' return will be determined by God the Father as well.

Now, back to our submission as wives: it's meant to be the same between husbands and wives to illustrate God's divine order. Wives submit to husbands just as the church submits to Jesus. In turn, husbands must submit to God the Father, as Jesus did His whole life even unto death.

But of course, real life is not always like that. And, I don't know about you, but wifely submission was a Biblical truth that I struggled with for years. Before we talk about keeping a marriage intact and saving one that's on the rocks, or what to do if you're married to an unbeliever, let's get the submission part out of the way.

Wifely Submission: Do I Have To?

In modern Western civilization, "submission" is a dirty word. The connotation in our minds is far closer to slavery than what the word actually means. Some dictionaries say the Greek term refers to military standing, something some of us might be uncomfortable with: He's the admiral, but I'm the captain.

However, when you look at the rest of the Bible, that's not all it means. Let's talk about how Jesus looked at submission:

They (Jesus and His disciples) came to Capernaum. When he was in the house, He asked them, "What were you arguing about on the road?" But they kept quiet because on the way they had argued about who was the greatest.

Sitting down, Jesus called the Twelve and said, "Anyone who wants to be first must be the very last, and the servant of all." — Mark 9:33-36 NIV

One of the great things about the gospels is that we get the picture of the perfect God-Man, Jesus interacting with twelve guys who are often incredibly human: selfish, foolish, self-serving, angry, unreasonable, etc. The fact is, we are just as human when we compare ourselves to the Lord's righteousness, so thank God He provided us these imperfect guides!

What I love about this scripture is that the apostles were too ashamed to admit to Jesus what they were arguing about. They already *knew* they were in the wrong. Think about that! Have you ever heard two guys squabble about who is better? Whose team is superior? Whose car is faster? Or even "did you see my man cave/gaming system/new TV"?

Before you lay this all at men's feet, women, I'm convicting you too. Have you ever compared yourself to other moms? Have you ever thought, "I may struggle with this, but at least I don't <fill in the blank> like *she* does!"

We've all done it at some point. Usually, we hide that fact from the people we respect because we know it's petty. We may even try to cover those sins away from God. But Jesus wasn't about to let the apostles get away with it either. In response to their squabbles, He made it clear that:

If you want to be first, you must be last.

No qualifiers, no excuse, no time limit. Just put everyone else first always, end of story.

But a little later in Mark, Jesus took this discussion to a bit of a different level:

Jesus called them together and said, "You know that those who are regarded as rulers of the Gentiles lord it over them, and their high officials exercise authority over them. Not so with you. Instead, whoever wants to become great among you must be your servant, and whomever wants to be first must be slave of all. For even the Son of Man did not come to be served, but to serve, and to give His life as a ransom for many." — Mark 10:42-45, NIV

Here, Jesus taught the apostles two powerful lessons on humility:

1. He explains the downside of being in control. While we often complain about submission, the fact is being in charge can go to our heads quickly, especially when we're not supposed to be. If you've read the gospels, you know that Jesus had little patience for the Jewish leaders of the day, the Pharisees. They were hypocritical, proud, arrogant, rich, and selfish, and they cared little for anyone who wasn't a Jew. But in this passage, Jesus was talking about Gentile rulers — the Romans. And as badly as you could talk about the Jewish leaders of His time, the pagan Roman leaders were far worse.

Basically, Jesus is saying that if you want to be great just for your own selfish desires, you are no better than a corrupt, unbelieving leader.

Yikes. We don't want to be that! Now, let's be clear here. He is not saying that leadership is wrong, but that true leadership comes from serving others without putting yourself first or bragging about your leadership.

2. Now, if that made the apostles — who'd just been bickering over "who is greater" — squirm, it was about to get a whole lot worse. Because then Jesus says that's why He came — not to be the type of leader who sits on a throne and gets his servants to cater to his whims, but a servant king, which is what He had been doing all along.
He came to Earth to *serve*.

For any of the disciples who didn't feel embarrassed by Jesus' earlier speech, they'd probably be covered in shame by now. I even sometime wonder if this is what started to get Judas off track. Can you even imagine his reaction to this statement?

I'm sure other disciples were confused, as well. They were raised to believe that the Messiah would be a warrior king who'd conquer Rome. They wouldn't grasp the full truth until receiving the Holy Spirit, but I bet it started a whole lot of discussion and debate

To put it all together, the God of the universe willingly left His Heavenly throne to serve us and to ultimately be tortured to death to bring us eternal life… and yet we question submitting to our husbands.

Now of course, not all spouses are the same. Not all are saved. Not all are kind. Not all treat us as they should, nor as the Bible commands. So please let me make a few things clear, first about duties, and then about abuse.

Submission and Caregiver Duties

First of all, when I'm talking about Godly submission to your husband, I'm not talking about being a doormat. A marriage is a partnership and a relationship. And there are many interesting schools of thought on who the primary earner should be and who should primarily take care of the kids.

The reality is that as parents of a child or children with challenges, both partners likely need to do a lot more work in caregiving and providing than they initially visualized. Lots of Christians take different approaches on this. For me, having my husband as head of the household means he earns most of the income — and he wants to — and I do most of the home maintenance. But he does help and often, and I earn a fair bit too. If there's a decision we are a 50/50 split on, it will likely go to him, but I can't even recall the last time that happened. I feel like we have a true partnership where we both thrive as we share our honest opinions and decisions.

An Abusive Spouse

Secondly, the submission I'm talking about is not anything resembling abuse and mistreatment. As much as the New Testament talks about a wife's role in marriage, it goes in even more depth about the husband's role. He is to be Christ-like toward us: gentle, kind, loving, and wanting the best for us.

He is supposed to help us avoid sin and protect us, guiding us, making the decisions on the hard calls that we disagree over.

If your husband in *any* way physically harms you or your children, I do not believe it is God's will that you stay. Remember, marriage is the image of Jesus' perfect union with the church. Abuse has no part of this. The way I see it, abuse fundamentally breaks the marriage contract, whether or not the abuser "claims" to be a Christian. No Godly woman should submit to abuse, nor allow her children to be abused.

If you are in this situation, please get help from an organization, your doctor, a trusted friend, your church, or anyone who can provide you with reliable help. Note: If your church insists you remain in a relationship where you are being physically abused, I encourage you to leave it and find a church that frees you from victimization and instead embraces you as a daughter of the Living God, worthy of respect, dignity, and safety.

And if your husband abuses you in a nonphysical matter, that may be grounds to leave as well, especially if he has an issue such as addiction, gambling, criminal behavior, cheating, etc. Please get advice and counseling if your husband is harming your family and prayerfully ask the Lord how He wants you to handle this situation.

Now here is the tricky part. You really do need to be incredibly open to the Holy Spirit's guidance. The Lord asked me to make a choice in my marriage that at least one church was against. Getting counseling is usually a wise idea. However, only the Spirit can guide you, and for that, you need to be in prayer and in the Word regularly.

Submission and a Husband's Disobedience

What do you do when your husband's opinion is at odds with God's work? When we talk about submission, we must remember that there is a Godly order to things. While your husband is the human you should put above all others, his decisions and choices do *not* trump God's will for your life. Your choices, may slightly differ, depending on whether or not your husband is a Christian.

What to Do If You're Married to a Nonbeliever

If your husband is not a believer, he will not be putting the Lord first. It is crucial that you tread very carefully regarding the Lord's will in all things. It can be easy for Christian wives in this situation to allow a sin pattern to be established in the home.

This also means that you are the spiritual head of your home. That is not God's perfect order, but a nonbeliever cannot be in this role. It means that you are responsible for nurturing the souls of your children and teaching them Godly principles. I was saved before my husband was, and I had to take this seriously. I believe Amelia and Zoe benefitted from what I taught them as children.

This will not be easy. You may be living in a home where non-Christian lifestyles and world views are embraced by your husband and modeled for your children. It is crucial that you pray over these situations regularly. I have witnessed firsthand how God can change a nonbelieving husband's heart right out of left field regarding sinful issues.

These sins may even include things you haven't considered or did not think were important before you followed Jesus. Challenges you may deal with in your home could include:

- Lack of respect for authority, especially God's authority
- Problems like envy, greed, cheating, and white lies
- Understanding generosity or tithing
- The importance of keeping holy the Sabbath or regular church attendance
- *Your* own need for Bible studies, prayer groups, and/or other forms of Christian fellowship
- Treating all people, even strangers, with a Christ-like attitude

In general, if your husband is not a Christian, he may not understand the value of Godly activities or behaviors. And as you grow in your Christian walk, that gap may grow.

Only God can bring salvation to your husband, but your prayers will make a difference. This is especially true if your husband is a tried-and-true atheist and actively fights against your Christian activities or input. I have been there. It was very painful. Believe me, Satan will do all he can to work against your marriage to a non-Christian. But God can save anyone, and He eventually brought my husband around after a few months of fervent prayer. During this time, I attended church, went to Bible studies, read my Bible in front of him, and prayed for his salvation every night. Even before his salvation, he became much gentler over time. Never underestimate the power of praying for a nonbelieving husband!

Additionally, while you want to maintain anything confidential that respects your husband's wishes, you may need to get some guidance or listen to the words of any Christian sister you know who is married to a nonbeliever. You have to tread a fine line between your husband's trust and confidence in you and getting the support you need.

However, as I said, I have seen God work on nonbelieving husbands to completely change their outlook from anti-God to attending church regularly. Never give up on this issue and never stop praying for your husband.

It's also especially important to model your behavior toward your husband in as much of a Christ-like manner as possible. The verses in 1 Peter 3:1-3 (ESV) discuss the impact of the Jesus-centered conduct of a Christian wife:

> Likewise, wives, be subject to your own husbands, so that even if some do not obey the word, they may be won without a word by the conduct of their wives when they see your respectful and pure conduct. Do not let your adorning be external—the braiding of hair and the putting on of gold jewelry, or the clothing you wear—

but let your adorning be the hidden person of the heart with the imperishable beauty of a gentle and quiet spirit, which in God's sight is very precious. For this is how the holy women who hoped in God used to adorn themselves, by submitting to their own husbands, as Sarah obeyed Abraham, calling him lord. And you are her children, if you do good and do not fear anything that is frightening.

A lot of people interpret this scripture to mean that women should not make themselves look good. I don't believe that verse means not to make yourself look good, especially for your husband. What it's really saying is that all the beauty treatments in the world aren't going to do a thing for your marriage if you are not treating your husband kindly and respectfully. Remember, I'm not saying to be a doormat but to approach him with thought and intention before engaging him.

The real meat of this scripture, however, is that the Resurrection power that God put inside you to demonstrate a Christ-like attitude can win over your husband for Jesus. Read that first verse again: "be subject to your own husbands, so that even if some do not obey the word, they may be won without a word by the conduct of their wives." Do what the Lord commands, and He will bless your prayers.

I went through a particularly contentious time with my husband when I was about five years into my salvation. I had gotten really fired up, was attending a home church, and was deep in scripture all the time. I can tell you that Satan did not like that! So, as to be expected, he played and preyed on my husband's attitude toward me.

We were fighting pretty regularly when my small group leader gave me that 1 Peter scripture above. I started to read it so much I memorized it. I clearly remember the first time I kept my mouth shut during a discussion that could have turned into an argument. I even remember where we *were* – in the car, which meant I had the freedom to get loud in an argument. My husband said something very inflammatory, and I bit my tongue to stay quiet. We had not even driven a block before he stopped talking.

The rest of the day was peaceful, and I was shocked! So I tried it again the next time. Before long, I was praying for God to hold my tongue. I wasn't always successful – I'm still not – but silence stops more fights than I ever thought possible! Actually, I credit the Holy Spirit for giving me the fortitude to weather those days.

Over time, things calmed down in our marriage. Shortly after that, I started working on my own acts of service for others, something I struggle with. I decided I'd start with my husband: making the daily coffee and serving him first. (As a coffee lover, this is a big deal!) He was surprised ... and delighted, even more so on day two and three, as he realized this was not just a "one off."

These two small actions, tiny acts of service and keeping quiet to avoid an argument went a long way. Little by little, he started to be less grumpy and less angry. He became calmer, and we started having real communication after that.

I'm happy to say that a few years later, he became a believer and regularly attends church with me now. It did, however, take a long time and a lot of prayer as well as a "never give up" attitude and faith that the Lord would handle it.

What To Do if You're Married to a Believer

If your husband is a believer, it doesn't mean there won't be marital strife. Raising children with disabilities puts a lot of stress on any marriage! But, there are things you can do when your believing husband is engaging in willful sins. Let's deal with them one at a time.

Submission: Yes, we are back on that topic again. Again, don't look at it as a dirty word. I'm not submitting on anything that compromises me, but rather, I'm respecting my husband's lead. When you give your husband the God-ordained leadership role in your home, he will realize that you respect him. When you serve him first, above your children, he will appreciate that. When you stop fighting and let him have some authority over matters that are important to him, he will start to feel better about himself. All these things go a long way to improving his walk with God, but they also lay the groundwork for you to share your heart with him. In 2017, my husband decided that he wanted both of us to join a gym that has military-style boot camps. I was dead set against any fitness regimen like this. But then he told me he wanted to do this not just because it appealed to him, but to do it together to strengthen our marriage. How could I resist?

With trepidation, I let him sign us up. The first class was one of the most difficult things I've ever done in my life, but it was also exhilarating. And it was so much fun to power through it together. I'm happy to say that now, years later, I'm in the best shape of my life, and I absolutely love our gym. And it's all thanks to submitting — and trusting — that he had it right.

Communication: When your husband sees that you respect and even trust him enough to lead, he will start listening to you more. I'm not saying he didn't accept my opinions before. We certainly have made choices based solely on my input in the past. However, the more leadership I give him, the more he trusts me when I have new ideas for helping our family, raising our kids, and even spending our money — one of the touchy topics in a marriage. This has made many areas of our life easier and given us both the feeling of being more of a team than ever before. One thing is more challenging: correcting him. Men struggle to receive spiritual correction from women, particularly their wives. That's why prayer is a crucial tool to help your husband's walk with God.

Prayer: Naturally, I pray for my husband, but I wanted to share how I pray for him. First, he is my first priority when I make my nightly prayers of supplication. I pray for him before the kids and before myself, unless I am praying for myself to become a better wife in general or to be the person he needs me to be to support him at that time. Next, rather than praying for what I want from him as a husband, I pray for what he needs, especially as it relates to his growth as a Christian. For years, I prayed that he would deeply, completely feel the love of the Lord in his life.

I also regularly pray that he will be surrounded with Christian men who can help in all the areas he needs, such as friendship and mentorship. Make sure you are praying that your husband gets the guidance and support he needs in his faith to grow and not stagnate. Finally, I pray for any of his daily struggles and challenges in critical areas, such as health, mental well-being, and fatherhood.

Intimacy: For many men, this is an important part of their life. As women, we go through ups and downs when we "feel" like being intimate with our husbands. The truth is there are times that we cannot, and there are times that we can but won't. There are stages of life where sex is easy and others when it can be difficult.

If you've stopped having any physical intimacy with your husband, it's time to bring it back. Sexual intimacy is one of the key elements that make marriage special and unique. I'm not going to write a comprehensive section on this because for those of us raising a child with severe autism, it can be difficult to find time and space for intimacy.

Pray for guidance on how to handle this, especially if you are in a time when you cannot physically have sex in a traditional way (i.e., post-pregnancy, menopause difficulties, health issues, etc.).

While there are other forms of intimacy that you can (and should) explore (i.e., hugging, kissing, holding hands), many men view sex as their favorite activity. It's important to find ways to make this work in your home in some form or other without violating your values. If you are really stuck getting this issue back on track, you may benefit from marriage counseling.

Become a team: As mentioned, my husband and I attend this gym that is based on the best military principles: work as a team-family, leave no one behind. Much of what I've learned is applicable to marriage.

At my gym, you are not alone. You have people pushing you and encouraging you.

We help each other overcome our most difficult obstacles, and believe me, there are some doozies in a workout!

That's how you need to think of your husband: as your *teammate* in life and definitely in parenting. God made two parents of different sexes for a reason, and your children need the influence of both of you especially for more challenging times.

The flipside is that your marriage is going to have a tough time being a positive influence if you are never "teammates." That is something you both are responsible for.

Bottom line: It doesn't matter where you are in your race—or in you walk with the Lord, or your husband's.

Devotionals every night? Wonderful. Only pray together for the kids? Great. Never ever prayed together. No problem. Everybody starts somewhere. If at least one of you follows the Lord and prays, fasts, and serves with a Christ-like heart, the other can come along someday, and what a beautiful day that will be!

Have you lifted, encouraged, or motivated your teammate, I mean husband, today? If not, this is something that you should consider doing every day!

This takes Godly wisdom, maturity, and the ability to honestly look at what's important, not just in our lives, but in our family as well. What door is God pushing you towards?

My husband and I have had our share of troubles but we always choose the door that says, "My marriage is what I will fight for!"

Chapter 11

Teaching Your Child the Gospel

*Teach them (Scriptures) to your children, talking about them when you sit
at home and when you walk along the road, when you lie down
and when you get up. – Deuteronomy 11:19, NIV*

If you're like me and your child has considerable intellectual delays, you may have spent some time thinking that he or she doesn't need the gospel and wouldn't understand it anyway. I remember thinking, *God will surely save my child!*

The problem, for me, is that I can't exactly be sure where my children lie on that intellectual spectrum. Nor do I know when the Lord would consider them fully capable of making that choice. It does seem to me that the older they get, the more they show some, if not a great deal, of understanding and maturity.

Even if your child cannot communicate or has severe delays in many areas, you can't be sure that an IQ score – or whatever you are using as a baseline to determine your child's intellectual maturity level – really shows how much or little he or she knows.

When I became convinced of this, I realized that no matter what, I need to be the one sharing the gospel with my children and letting the Lord soak understanding into them.

This is even more important today. The world we live is determinedly set against the gospel. The Bible refers to Satan as "the prince of this world" (John 12:31), "the ruler of this world" (Ephesians 2:2), and the "god of this world" (2 Corinthians 4:4). Keep in mind that any power Satan has comes from God. And as believers we are protected to the extent of our ability to avoid temptation or giving the devil a foothold, but unbelievers can be caught in the snares of his schemes. We too can succumb when we wander out from the Lord's protection, falling prey to temptation and sin.

But the most convincing argument I can say to you is that if you don't teach your children the Lord's values, the world will creep in and teach them things that are counter to Jesus' teachings. It does not matter what special program they are in. The culture is seeking on every level to share unbiblical principles to every community, regardless of age, race, or ability. Your only defense is to be proactive in this area and teach your child as best you can.

The fact is, kids who struggle with communication may in fact know more than we can tell, until we see evidence of it.

I have been there! Around the time of middle school, my oldest daughter accomplished her first lie. A few years later, she actually told a fairly complex lie in high school, at a skill level I did not think she had. So never doubt that your child can understand far more than he or she reveals.

Teaching your autistic child about the gospel can be challenging. However, I have found ways to give my kids a solid foundation in God's Word.

How to Get Started

Teaching is difficult for me but that's not the only hurdle I had to overcome. Neither of my children enjoys reading or doing worksheets. Zoe and Amelia both have great difficulty listening to me, in particular. But once I was convinced that this was my God-given duty, I had to find ways to overcome these difficulties with the Lord's help. And for a time, I was their only Christian parent. At that point, I was solely responsible for their spiritual development so I again found my inspiration from mothers in the Bible.

The first mother that inspired me was Jochebed, Moses' birth mother. She took extraordinary risks to save her child's life. Her early direction paved the way for God to later raise him to become the greatest leaders in the Old Testament. As mothers who are struggling, let's see how her story can encourage us.

The Faith of Jochebed

We don't know much about Jochebed from the Bible, but all three of her children were born when the Israelite nation was under Egyptian rule. During her third pregnancy, the Pharaoh of the day had decreed that *all* Hebrew babies be put to death immediately. Can you imagine the terror for expecting couples? The fear that must have crept into families all over the country?

Into this holocaust, Moses was born, and like any loving mother, Jochebed looked at him and fell in love. At great personal risk, she kept him hidden but by the age of three months, he was not quiet enough to hide anymore. She put him in a makeshift boat to float him down the river. We don't know if she was told to do this directly by God, but we can trust that this plan was divinely inspired. Still, think about what courage and trust it took for her take send away her "beautiful child" (Exodus 2:2) and leave a helpless baby totally in God's hands. Yikes! I remember all the years I wouldn't even let go of my daughters' hand. But she bravely did what she had to to save his life.

The story does not end there, of course. Moses floated down the river and was picked up by Pharaoh's daughter who also took to him – possibly because she wanted an heir to the throne. She likely guessed that this was a Hebrew baby and decided to raise the child anyway. Moses' sister, Miriam, had followed the basket down the river and witnessed the woman plucking it from the shores. She spoke to her and offered her the services a Hebrew wet nurse — Moses' true mother, Jochebed.

Pharaoh's daughter agreed to pay her to nurse the baby. In this way, Jochebed got her baby back until he was weaned. It must have been with mixed feelings of joy and sacrifice that she knew her baby would be safe, that she got to bond with him for a few short years, and that she would have to surrender him permanently at some point.

What can we learn from Jochebed's story?

Lesson 1: Godly love for your child is rewarded. Jochebed had such great love for her child that she would do anything to save her boy. God rewarded her by sending him back to her arms, if only for a brief time. He rescued Moses, protected him, and ultimately chose him as the man to save the Israelites from slavery in Egypt. When you think about teaching your child in spite of your shortcomings or their limitations, let your love for him or her be your guide. I don't think my girls will grow up to save a nation, like Moses did, but I do know that they are loving young ladies who always surprise me with their kindness and joyfulness.

We'll never know how much Jochebed knew about Moses' future, but Miriam did, and she surely shared that information.

Lesson 2: Your trust in God will be fulfilled. Jochebed could not have known what would happen when she put Moses in the river. The Nile runs through the location of where the Israelites lived, Goshen, and eventually flows north into the Mediterranean Sea. Pharaoh's daughter lived downstream, and Jochebed must have known he would pass by the royal dwelling. He could have been easily killed if that little basket had capsized or the Egyptian guards discovered him. Or he could have been lost at sea. But Jochebed completely trusted that God would protect him.

I'm sure their parting was painful, but how blessed she must have been to nurse him, even just for a brief period, when so many families around her were in mourning. Her faith and trust in God's plan were fulfilled.

In the same way, if you are faithful in teaching God's Word to your children, He will be faithful to protect those seeds you plant in them, even if you don't think they understand. Sometimes, I will see Zoe or Amelia do something that's come from those teachings, like recalling a scripture verse or never eating without saying grace first. This is how sharing the gospel can manifest in your autistic child.

Lesson 3: You can do this even if you have nothing. Jochebed was a woman in a nation of slaves or servants, who were at the whim of Pharaoh. She had very little in the way of worldly possessions, and certainly there were no holy texts yet, since Moses himself wrote the first five books of the Bible. How did Moses come to question his station in life and eventually follow the Lord God?

I like to think that all that time that Jochebed nursed Moses (probably around age three or four), she spoke to him about the Lord and His great love and mercy in saving Moses. I know that's what I would do! You need nothing to teach your kids, just your own strong faith, values, and a Bible, a tool Jochebed did not have.

God had great plans for Moses. He set the Israelites free, gave them the Ten Commandments, and led them through the desert to the Promised Land. Jochebed set down the basics, and the Lord provided a rich, full education when Pharaoh's daughter picked him up. Because of God's great provision, Moses had all the tools he needed to write those five Bible books and lead a nation.

In our home, it costs nothing to say grace, pray with the girls most every night, read scripture to them, or play Christian music. What regular things can you do to create a Godly atmosphere in your home?

Seven Tips to Help You Teach Your Kids about God

Throughout the story of this Biblical mother, God shows us that with faith, courage, and love, we can teach our children what they need to become a believer who serves God's purpose. These tips may help you:

1. Be creative.

Music is a great tool to reach so many of our kids on the autism spectrum. Plus it's a wonderful way to memorize scriptures. Even though I always feel intimidated by this, I created a little song for Zoe based on part of James 1:17. Here are the words if you want to use them:

> Every good and perfect gift, good and perfect gift, Comes from Father God above, Father God above, Who gives gifts in perfect love, gifts in perfect love from…. (This is where I have Zoe yell or sing "God!")

When Zoe was little, I would sing this tune and drum on her arm or belly. Eventually, we learned the tune by rotating it through different instruments that I would "imitate." I would toot like horn or go "plink, plink, plink" for the piano. Then we'd get back to the verse after we'd gone through several instruments.

Writing words comes naturally to me, but writing songs doesn't. For me, it's fun to try to make up word or memory games to remember verses. What is your gift or talent? Pray that God helps you use it to creatively inspire your children to memorize verses.

2. Try different things.

Getting that verse set to music and making a game of it only happened because everything else I had tried at the time failed: Christians books, stories, reading, apps, videos, you name it. Sometimes the only thing you can be certain of is when your child is not interested, so you need to keep on plugging in different things to help them learn about the faith, just as if you are teaching math to a kid who doesn't get it. Try *anything* you can think of to reach your kids.

Here are some more creative ideas to get you started:

- Christian kids' apps, like Biblical coloring apps
- Books made specifically for kids, like pop-up books.
- Christian comic books or graphic novels
- Printable worksheets found online. These were great for my girls!
- Homeschool tools, resources, and curriculum (even if you don't homeschool)
- Coloring pages
- Arts and crafts with a Biblical message
- Picture books with scripture verses
- Biblical toys (i.e., Noah's ark, nativity sets)
- Christian videos like Veggie Tales
- Decorative scripture art to hang in their rooms

3. Sacrifice to serve them spiritually.

It had been on my heart to get my girls into a church that can serve them. At the time, I'd been attending a home church with beloved friends. This blessed and taught me so much, but despite their best efforts, they could not think of a way to accommodate my children.

I was very reluctant to leave, but when God called me out shortly after, I knew I had to comply. My family needed church more than I did. I found a church that could meet their needs in childcare and teach them about Christ.

This was incredibly difficult, and I didn't want to do it. However, getting back into a church actually brought my husband along a path where he could find the Lord and salvation. What sacrifice is God asking you to make in order to teach your child?

4. Start memorizing scripture.

My kids don't like to read, and when I'm fumbling to find verses in the kids' Bible, I lose ground fast. But I can easily share verses I've memorized, and that goes a long way towards training a child who does not want to read. Start with something simple, like John 3:16, Luke 6:31, or the Lord's Prayer, and grow from there.

5. Repeat, repeat, repeat.

Ask any parent who's on their 1,000th viewing of "Frozen": Autistic kids frequently enjoy lots of repetition! Years of Bible study has taught me that you only get to know scripture well when you go over it, over and over. A good way to do this is for your child to pick a single theme and drop a few simple scriptures into the reference.

For example, I reviewed "light" scriptures in the Bible and after just a few weeks, my daughter learned that:

- God created light. (Genesis 1:3)
- God is the father of lights. (James 1:17)
- Jesus is the light of the world. (John 8:12)
- Scripture is a lamp for our feet, a light on our path. (Psalm 119:105)
- We can pray, "The Lord is our light" (Psalm 27:1) when we are troubled.

As mentioned, I was already doing James 1:17 in musical verse so the first scripture I chose was easy. Then I picked few more from study and plus Genesis 1:3 (on light) for good measure.

6. *Teach what you know.*

That whole "light" lesson came about because one day at Bible study, we were studying in depth that Jesus is the light of the world. We were also studying Genesis, so I took the opportunity to add the creation story as a lesson too. The Holy Spirit put these ideas in my head after attending that study. In that, way Zoe and Amelia learned to associate God with light.

What are you learning in Bible study? If you are not attending one in person, or cannot, I encourage you to find one that you can do at home, either a devotional or an online study.

If you're already studying God's Word, pray for the Holy Spirit to inspire you to share what you have learned and discovered with your child.

7. *Read scripture aloud.*

This may sound pretty simple, but just reading scripture out loud allows the Lord to plant seeds in their minds. You can do this in a number of ways. Here is what I have done:

- Share a Bible story or verse during dinner.
- Read one or two Psalms out loud in the morning. If I'm rushed, I set my Bible app to read it for me.
- Recite verses you've memorized while doing chores around them.
- Read scripture over your children when they are sick, fussy, or upset.

Scripture spoken aloud doesn't have any special "magical" ability, but it can nourish your entire home, the way a healthy meal does your body good. In fact, my unbelieving husband was hearing the Word too!

8. *Keep praying with faith.*

None of this would have happened had I not been praying for my daughters nightly for years, including asking God *how* I could teach them. I knew I had to teach, and I knew, also, that I was not equipped for it at all. But God is faithful for prayers like this and will give you exactly what you need to lead your children in learning about Jesus.

Before you teach them, pray that God will set His Word in your child's heart and allow it to take root. Pray He will give you the lessons He wants them to learn. God will bless our best efforts, even if our kids can't read, sit still, communicate, or acknowledge what they have heard.

The Bible teaches us that Moses himself stuttered; yet on occasion after occasion, he stood up to Pharaoh, to the nation when they sinned, and to rebellions within the nation. He did this because he trusted God to help his words despite his fears. Never doubt that God can use your words to reach your child or that your child can win souls!

Kids with severe challenges and disabilities need to know and understand God's Word as much as any other child, and it's your duty to figure out how to do that in a way they can digest. That's *all* you need to do: Make sure they hear it as best they can. God will do the rest.

Imagine my joy when at prayers one night when I asked my daughter, "God is the father of??" and she said, "Light!" I could feel the Lord smiling down on us. If I can do it, you can too!

Chapter 12

Approaching Education

Train up a child in the way he should go: and when he is old, he will not depart from it. – Proverbs 22:6, NKJV

For kids with learning challenges, behavioral issues, and other issues that go hand-in-hand with autism, school can be the biggest hurdle to overcome. There are numerous options for children today. Some may solve all your problems, some may not, and sometimes you have to change from one to the other. Here is a review of these options and what you need to know.

Before I dive in though, I'd like to share a few words about inclusion.

Inclusion and Special Education

You have hopefully heard a lot about "inclusion" in terms of special education. The fact is it has different definitions and meanings, depending on whom you talk to. For me, inclusion specifically means having disabled children attend class, recess, and school activities with their peers. This means they are doing similar classwork alongside their peers, working with other students, and getting support at a level appropriate to them. By "similar," I mean that if the class is learning about planets, your child is also learning about planets.

Not every school will define inclusion like this. In fact, some schools and administrators will call your child's presence in a classroom "inclusion" even if they are not interacting with peers or doing any of the same work. For example, for one of my daughters, inclusion consisted of coming into the kindergarten class in exchange for candy for a few minutes a day. Meanwhile, at lunch she'd be alone with her aide, crying.

Classroom inclusion is a tool that can help your child to see, learn, and model age-appropriate behavior. If your child is only with other children on the autism spectrum, they cannot see and mimic how their peers act and react. They will only get direction from the adults in charge.

Personally, I do not believe that this is an ideal situation, particularly in elementary school. It took my daughter a long time to actually notice her peers, but once she did, she desperately wanted to participate with them. My favorite example of inclusion was the time her fourth grade teacher allowed her to do a math problem on the blackboard. She got it right, and the other kids were excited! They had no idea she could do math like that. It was a learning experience for everyone.

When you segregate students with disabilities, other students, especially when they are young, get the message that these kids are different. This can be misinterpreted as having less value, especially if students are not used to seeing kids with different disabilities in their day-to-day life.

On the other hand, there can be times where you'd prefer to have your child segregated, at least for a time. This can include challenges such as head banging, soiling their pants, severe self-injury, aggression toward other children, and more. This may be putting your child at more risk of judgment, bullying, and harsh punishment or worse, if you do include them.

As you can see, choosing inclusion for your child is not always a clear or simple decision to make. It depends on the school, the grade, staffing, and more.

A year later, my child had regressed and graduated out of the charter school environment into a public school. In this new school, there was no longer a safe environment available that met her needs since this traditional public school did not endorse true inclusion. We felt she was safer in an autistic support classroom for the duration of middle and high school.

Because I've experienced both the good and bad of public and charter schools, I'd like to share what I've learned to help you choose the best environment for your child.

Public Schools

The downside to public schools is that as of this writing, the quality of a public school tends to depend on the location of that school. How much funding does your area's public school get for special education?

Even if your school gets a good amount of funding specifically for special needs education, there is no way of knowing if that will continue as the school boards shifts or if it will be spent on systems or supports that benefit your child. For example, our current district is fairly wealthy and puts a sizable amount of our budget into special education programs. However, there have been times when elected board members wanted to reduce and re-appropriate some of this funding. This is always a challenge with school boards, and it's one of the reasons why you may want to consider getting involved with your district's school board meetings. (Obviously, that's a time-consuming item to add to your duties so another good option is to friend a parent who already regularly attends and will keep you in the loop.)

Public School Benefits

You might not find enough support for your autistic student in a poorly funded district and maybe not at all in a failing or understaffed school district. It's important to consider this as well when choosing to send your child to public school, if you have a choice. Charter schools, cyberschool, or homeschool may be better solutions in terms of some of these resources if your district is struggling financially.

Well-funded public schools provide benefits such as:

Plenty of resources for special needs. Our local school district has enough funding to house things like a sensory room, special classrooms, additional classes, trips and tours focused on community integration, skill-building for disabled kids, and more. For example, Zoe's high school has a sensory room that she can visit when she needs to unwind, which has been helpful to get her through her school day. Our high school has also partnered with numerous state and local-based programs that allow kids to experience vocational training, job-site instruction, group living facilities, and targeted college education programs for students with special needs.

Quality tenured staff. If you're worried about high staff turnover, public school can be a desirable choice. Some teachers have been in the field for a decade or more. While you might have more turnover with aides than teachers, and with teachers than case workers, you'll probably have a steadier staff because public schools often pay better than charter schools. Additionally, you may have more therapeutic staff available (speech, physical therapy, and occupational therapy), also with less turnover. You may even have special education staffing specifically for specials, such as adaptive gym. These teachers and aides have often been very helpful since they have been trained in your child's issues.

More accountability. When we moved our kids from a charter school to a public school, we had to sue our former school. Through our attorney, we discovered that many of the IEPs the charter school had written were technically incorrect as per legal standards. Not all of them — it depended on who was in charge and who was doing the writing. This changed from year to year, including staff member and the positions available. That happens less often in a traditional public school.

Public school also provided more formal procedures for things like grievances, complaints, and more. We personally had an easier time with these challenges in public school than with the charter school.

Tailored teaching. Public school special education teachers tend to be trained specifically in special education and/or autism support. You may be surprised what non-special ed teachers do not know about supporting a student on the autism spectrum.

Possibility of more intimate and targeted education. You may have access to full-time paraprofessionals available who can provide your child one-on-one support and/or smaller classroom sizes. Our public school also has resources for special classes, such as adaptive gym, so that kids are not forced to integrate in these physically demanding classes.

These benefits are best-case scenarios, by the way, and again, are very money-centered. Turnover is higher in poorer districts. Therapeutics, paraprofessionals, and other services may be scarcer, too.

Public School Problems

Let's look at some of the top challenges of public school.

Little to no support for inclusion. Public schools tend to look inclusion like a head scratcher. If you have a school that is not intentionally including special needs kids all along, it may be too late. Those students already see our children as "other."

Make no mistake, the old theory of "they have recess (or lunch) together" does not work. 100+ kids in a cafeteria or schoolyard is not inclusion.

Rigidity of teaching. Your child learns differently. That's great! But it's likely that will not be viewed favorably in public school. Many administrators just want your child to measure up to certain standards. Period. If it's not measurable by their yardstick, like standardized testing, it doesn't count.

A child with a high IQ but a high level of communication, behavioral, and social challenges and distractions will often be taught as if they have a low IQ, and in turn, fall below grade level (a decade or more). They may be given coursework far below their capabilities.

Strict adherence to testing. One of the reasons there's so much rigidity is that public schools tend to be uber-focused on tests and measurement. Your child could seem to have a low IQ even if the problem actually flows from the test, the atmosphere, stress, or even fluorescent lights. (Yes, that can be a huge problem!) As one teacher told me, "Well, if she can't answer the questions, how do I know she knows the work?" The answer is that there are other ways for her to demonstrate what she knows, but our staff didn't believe it. That has caused many difficulties in our daughter's education.

Difficulty with disputes. We've had our share of difficult disputes with charter schools, but simply employing an advocate or lawyer usually allowed us to be treated fairly. A public school, however, has far more power and legal representation. It will be more difficult to get justice or fairness when you are dealing with them, even with experts on your side.

Few outdoors or field trip experiences. In public school, my kids get twenty minutes of recess a day. That's it. They also rarely get field trips—a few per year. Of course, every charter school is different, but this was very different from nature hikes several times a week and up to one field trip per school month.

Parental input may be discouraged. Public schools have curriculum planned down to the level where they know what students are doing, where, when, and how for every moment of the day. There's little room for creative engagement outside of specials and strict adherence to mandated curriculum. Sometimes even outdated methods and a heavy reliance on testing are also emphasized, leaving parents little input in creating a teaching plan that works best for how their children learn.

While I did say that IEPs tend to be more organized, make no mistake, the process can be just as complex and challenging as in charter school. Explaining your child's capabilities in an IEP meeting can get you the "you're not the expert" look. You may not have the flexibility to get the curriculum you'd prefer in public school.

Your child may be more at risk. Now, it is true that a child can be bullied or abused, by either students or staff, at any school. But because public school staffers have more secure tenure and embedded reputations, the wrong person in the right position dealing with can be a long-term challenge. Sadly, it's more likely that an entrenched public school teacher, aide, or administrator will get away with bullying or other unpleasant tactics. And of course, public schools can be hotbeds for crime depending on where you are located, what kind of security they have, and existing rules or policies such as who is allowed in the bathroom. Be fully aware of these issues before enrolling your child.

Improving Your Public School

If your only option is a public school, you'll need to either do something completely different or make the best of it. What can you do to make a public school work for your child?

- Create your own ideal school plan for your child. Now, you probably won't get this plan 100 percent approved, but it's a good starting point for negotiations during IEP plans and 504 meetings.
- Have a special needs advocate. I never go to a meeting without my advocate. I'm fortunate that we have a local advocacy organization, and this service is free of charge. That might not be the case for you, so investigate what your special education advocacy options are for your most important meetings, encounters, or disputes.
- Bring in an inclusion expert. There are companies that train your school how to be fully inclusive and abide by ADA laws. We used such an expert in our charter school, but I've heard great things have been done in public schools as well. A word of caution: These teams need to be in place nearly a year before school starts and may have limited capacity to take on schools. Don't hesitate to research this option.
- Be kind. Your child's team at school should not be your enemy. They are doing their best with limited resources. While it is true that there are always bad apples (we have been there), you do have options. Certain staff members may not have to participate or you can request an alternate. That said, don't start off in an antagonistic manner. Do your best to work together.

Charter School Benefits

Our children attended charter school for elementary, and for my oldest, part of middle school, and now are in public middle and high school. Initially, our chosen charter school was a wonderful selection. The benefits we saw included:

Extremely flexible support for inclusion. Charter schools and inclusion often go hand-in-hand. This is one of the top reasons parents of kids with disabilities (or gifted children) will choose one. We had to actually teach it to them, but the same was true of public school. That said, once they embraced it, my kids were given a great outlet. And because of the school's flexibility, we got unique options that wouldn't work in a traditional public school, like covered lights in the main classroom.

Specialized curriculum. Based on an environmental mission, a huge draw to this school was daily or at least weekly hikes and outdoor excursions. These trips embraced the mission of the school and provided lots of real-world learning opportunities. Look for charter schools that embrace your values and your child's passions.

Hands-on experience. Charter schools are more open to creative ways of teaching that don't necessarily involve over testing. Much of the work my kids did was hands-on and highly immersive. The nearby pond was a frequent area for science class, and local historic homes were sites for social studies or history classes. The school even kept its own beehives. Plus, most classrooms had a mascot. Zoe had the job of feeding the class guinea pig in fifth grade. This type of instruction offered multiple ways to evaluate what my kids learned outside of testing.

Potential for better parental/community involvement. Parents were welcome to participate in frequent volunteer opportunities and other activities. Our charter hosted community-building events during school hours like holiday feasts, morning meetings, mystery readers, and a classroom coordinator. I was onsite at school much of the school year when my daughters were little.

There were plenty of field trips that involved the local community, like businesses, the mayor's office, or utility providers. There was even a community service project to rake leaves for local families. The first grade did a "farm tour," visiting eight local farms in as many weeks. That was one of Zoe's favorite school years!

Great flexibility. Forget rigid seats in rows. Sit on the floor, sit on a donut, sit on a yoga ball, sit where you like, or stand if you prefer. Not every time for every class, but often enough that the kids rarely felt stiff. Yet again, this sort of option means charter schools and inclusion go well together.

Creative programming. Charter schools often create unique and engaging learning opportunities that public schools don't. Our school took part in Responsive Classroom, which was great for students. They emphasized that students "see" each other as a way to build respect and reduce bullying. The academic curriculum was called EIC -Environment as an Integrating Context for Learning, which integrates community, nature, student-led projects, and more into every subject, giving kids plenty of reinforcement while learning about the world around us. For example, Zoe often enjoyed the trips to the pond for observing frogs for science class.

Charter School Problems

Every good thing in this broken world has issues too. Here's what we experienced:

No or few after-school clubs or sports. There were attempts at extra-curricular activities, but the only one I know that lasted was Girls on the Run, which was coordinated by outside parties. Even if they had, unlike public school, my kids' aides would not have been able to accompany them, so after-school clubs were nonexistent for my kids.

High staff turnover. That includes teachers and administrators. It made it for an inconsistent couple of years. The sad part is that some really good people left, and the final shake out of the administration was actually quite disappointing. They definitely contributed to the rocky finale to our charter school journey.

Detrimental parent involvement. While it was great to have a lot of input on how my daughters were taught and included, some parents abused this sort of involvement by changing the curriculum. They wanted to change the layout of the school in a way that made it *less* friendly to students with learning challenges and more conducive to prepping their kids for college. (This was elementary school, by the way.)

Unfortunately, this had both short- and long-term repercussions on the quality of the school and its treatment of students.

Lack of resources for grievances. If you had a complaint, you'd formally file it, but at times, the person in charge of this was complicit in the very thing you were complaining about. In a small community, it also meant that everyone knew everyone's business, and complainers could be ostracized.

Lack of fiscal accountability. This is common in charter schools. From embezzlement to misappropriation, money could be siphoned from where it was expected to go. Because public charter schools get less funding than traditional public schools and are more or less on their own with accounting, there is temptation to lie and cheat with the budget.

Solutions that hurt children. When our school decided to discontinue the middle school that was in the approved charter, they created a narrative about how "bad" it was. They brought that narrative to life by staffing it with new teachers, refusing to support them, and refusing to replace teachers and key staff who quit. In other words, they manipulated the environment to make middle school educationally ineffective and unsafe, so they could justify cutting it out. I could go on and on here, but let's just say that God's grace and several good people who cared kept my older daughter safe that last year of middle school.

Ignoring bullying issues. Because charters need to be renewed, administrators like to pretend that everything is wonderful even when it's not. Now, I know that pretending bullying doesn't occur also happens in public school, but here there is financial motive to cover it up too. The most frequent problems I heard at that parent's group were either mishandling or completely ignoring a child's complaint of bullying, even if it was frequent. This was especially true if the bully's parent was well-connected.

Ableism and racism. In our last year at our school, I saw kids with disabilities and kids with darker skin treated differently than other students. It was gut-wrenching, and everyone was afraid to even bring it up.

Why I Skipped Private Schools and Homeschooling

Although these options were available, I decided not to choose either of these options for my children.

Private School

There are very few people I even know who send their child to a private school and with good reason: You have to pay tuition in addition to footing your own IEP bills. This can double your out-of-pocket tuition.

However, there are private schools that are meant for kids with special challenges that help them to mainstream. The tuition is about the same as private plus IEP costs in my state, so this is another option you'll have to weigh carefully.

Homeschooling and Unschooling

I know parents with children on the autism spectrum who homeschool, unschool, or attend a cyberschool or co-op. Under the right conditions, these are wonderful options. If your child went through the Covid-19 lockdowns and did well with their education while at home, or was successful with remote learning, this might well be an option for you.

If your child did not fare well, I highly recommend you talk to parents who are homeschooling a child on the spectrum and see how it is going for them. Then you can weigh how you feel about trying it. This could be more challenging if your child is not responsive to you or if you have a difficult time remaining disciplined.

While I wanted to go this route, those last two sentences describe our family. And Zoe struggled during lockdown. With prayer and discernment, I realized this was not the right route for my family.

That said, as my daughter is now approaching higher grades, I wonder if homeschooling would have been a better choice had we started when our children were in elementary school. Today, more than five million Americans homeschool their children, and many have children with special challenges that the public school system did not properly address.

Additionally, public schools today are adding programming that may not sit well with a Christian parent. If you send your child, I advise you to carefully look over the curriculum beforehand. If the school is resistant to show you what they are teaching your child, consider that a red flag.

I recommend you find people who have taken these routes to fully explore your options for educating your child.

Resources for Homeschooling, Co-ops, Unschooling, and Cyber Schools

Kids can thrive with alternative education. If you are new and this seems overwhelming but you want to try it, look for a local Christian homeschooling co-op that fits your values. For example, many people in my church homeschool and share resources while others attend a formal co-op that allows children access to a standard curriculum and opportunities such as group field trips.

Laws on homeschooling vary from state to state, so I recommend you check out the Home School Legal Defense Association state law resource page at https://hslda.org/laws. Connect with other local parents who have homeschooled or unschooled in the last few years as well to get up-to-date information about what kind of challenges you might encounter along the way.

You can also check the resources at Unschoolers Online for more info on both homeschooling and unschooling. Look for local support groups on their site: http://www.unschoolers.com/supportgroups.html.

Cyber schools are another solution we have not tried but that has proved helpful for kids I've known who have had less severe challenges. Do your research to see if any are available in your area.

Chapter 13

The IEP

If any of you lacks wisdom, he should ask God, who gives generously to all without finding fault, and it will be given to him. – James 1:5, Berean

Getting Your Child's Education Right with the IEP

Individualized Education Plan meetings (IEPs) can be a huge source of stress for parents of kids on the autism spectrum. However, they are a valuable tool to ensure that your child gets the education he or she deserves. I have been through years of these meetings: some good, some bad, and some that had me crying on the drive home. At one point, IEP day used to bring me nothing but anger and frustration. It seemed like my kids were not getting the quality education they should have, but today, I no longer struggle as much.

Part of this is has been due to dedication of the teachers and other staffers over the years, but part of it is also letting go and letting God take over. At one point, I considered nothing to be more important than full inclusion and firmly believed that the primary function of school was to help my child excel as much as possible academically. Other times, I believed that school was more of a social outlet where my kids could and should meet other disabled peers, who will make up the bulk of their relationships.

At varying times, schools are useful in different ways for our children. And even if school does not provide our kids what we hoped, there are still other ways to help them have satisfying, productive lives.

Now, let's look at a typical IEP and how you can optimize it to benefit your child.

The IEP Process and Meeting

IEP meetings are regular meetings (every one to two years or when you request them) that occur at your school, either in person or virtually. Attendees include the parents of the student, the student if he or she is able, at least one regular education teacher, the child's special education teacher or team (at least one), a representative from the school district who is knowledgeable about special education (not necessarily from the school), someone such as a school psychologist who can share test results, your child's case worker if they have one, and other individuals who have other expertise. For example, if your child has any therapists or attends a special education gym class, those professionals may attend as well.

Your child might have a paraprofessional or an IA, and they may be part of the IEP — or not. Often, they will be out supporting your child, at other times, they may provide important data. It depends on many things. Ideally, your child will have a caseworker who administrates and coordinates the details of your child's IEP and case. And of course, your child can and should attend if he or she is able.

As you can see, this can quickly add up to a lengthy line of people from the district against you and your child, all alone on the other side of the table. When I first started out, I did whatever I could to make sure my husband came with me so I would not be alone, but he was usually not available to attend.

Fortunately, you are allowed to bring your own support, which we had in the form of a special education advocate. A good advocate will be in your child's corner. They have a firm grasp of the IEP process and special education law and knowledge of the district and, hopefully, the players involved.

A great advocate will have years of experience under their belt, has worked with the school your child attends (public or charter), understands your child's needs and disability, and will be with your family for the long haul. A really great advocate is a trustworthy steward of your child's rights who will also know how to calm people on both sides of the table and aid in sound negotiation to help your child thrive.

If all this sounds more like a day at a lawyer's office than a school meeting, you're right. It's been my experience that I want the best education for my kids while the school wants "what they always do" to be the right choice. Most of the time, a fair IEP meeting will come down in the middle of that. However, a good foundation of education and groundwork can help your IEP go smoothly if you are honest with several things:

- **Where your child is academically**. If he or she is struggling through a health issue, difficulties at home, stressful situations, a change that may be unexpected (a different school, room, or teacher), onset of puberty, or even something that you can't quite put your finger on, this may not be the time to fight for inclusion, advanced academics, or other academic goals that may have been low-hanging fruit in the past.
- **Your school's ability to accommodate**. While some items are deal breakers (i.e., ensuring your child is not given food that trigger negative behaviors), you will still likely have to work within your school's budget, experience, and limitations. As mentioned earlier, budgets only go so far depending on your district, but the Individuals with Disabilities Education Act (IDEA) guarantees disabled students in the American public school system the right to a Free Appropriate Public Education (FAPE) in the Least Restrictive Environment (LRE). If you believe that your child is not getting his or her needs met under this law, you can hire a special education advocate or lawyer to help.

- **Guidance from the Lord:** God doesn't want you to fight every battle every time. You need time in prayer, scripture, and silence for direction about what and how to fight for with your child's educators, if at all.

Once you have a firm understanding of these basics, here is what you need to know to get the best possible outcome within reason for your child's education:

Know Your Rights

The Americans with Disabilities Act (ADA) and IDEA exist to protect the rights of people with disabilities, and that includes your autistic child. For example, did you know that students with celiac disease are protected under the ADA? Even if your child has not (or not yet) been diagnosed with a disability that requires services, you should research what provisions can be made for your child's needs. What has been done for other students in the area in the past, even in a different school, and what can be done now? A great resource is the Wright's Law website at http://wrightslaw.com/. In addition to knowing federal disability laws, you should also understand your state laws as well. Finally, do not forget that when the rights of people with disabilities are trampled upon or are neglected, it is a civil rights or legal issue. You may need to secure a lawyer in that case. If so, it's wise to hire an attorney who has experience in disability and/or special education cases.

Get Special Training

Ever heard of the *Gaskin* case? It's a 1990s lawsuit that took place in Pennsylvania when inclusion and the least restricted environment were not yet well-enforced or addressed in this state. This case set a precedent that a lawyer can use to sue to get appropriate services for your child if you feel he or she is not being fairly or properly included in their current school year. I'm not sure if *Gaskin* applies to other states, although I know a similar law also is in effect in New York. Remember that an appropriate education also includes speech, physical, and occupational therapy services, if required. If a doctor has determined your child needs such therapies and your child does not receive them, you can sue for damages, especially if the school year has ended. Schools and therapists need to provide proof of this service, and if they cannot, your child is entitled to reimbursement so you can pursue those services yourself. Learn what information you need to know. Contact your local special education services resource, mental health department, or other organizations that focus on supporting students with disabilities or specific needs, such as an advocacy center or an autism resource center. Ask if they have specific training designed for parents to have effective IEP meetings that benefit the student.

Get Appropriate Data

You may need to ask for specific tools or data before stepping into that IEP meeting. From my experience, charter schools, especially new ones, can be extremely disorganized with data processing, such as progress during speech therapy. On the other hand, a public school may have you drowning in figures and measurements at the meeting. More is always better than less! No matter how much data is available, be sure to ask for it.

Additionally, make sure that it is provided in a readable, easy-to-understand format. For example, speech therapists can provide graphs that plot out how your child is doing with the therapy. This allows you to easily see whether or not he or she is making progress. Lack of progress is a red flag that the current approach is not working and should be changed.

Next, make sure the data is clearly organized. If you see results for two separate rubrics mixed together (like how your child is doing on separate sight word lists), ask for them to be pulled apart. Data should be taken regularly and numbers/percentages tracked against the IEP goal ("answered properly 10 out of 20 times"). You need to see your child's name, the goal, where data is collected, and how. If you believe that data is not being properly tracked, make that specific request in your IEP. Finally, if behaviors are repetitively occurring, you can ask for a functional behavioral analysis (FBA) to be put in place. From there, you can collaborate with your caseworker to develop a Positive Behavior Support plan if they have one in place. Ask for this in an email, so that there is a paper trail and make sure to copy anyone who represents your child.

Keep Those Graphs Moving Up

One of the most important things I learned is that a child should always be progressing toward their goals. Ask to use bar graphs in IEP documentation so that you can see if that line is moving up. If it's not, then you need to make changes, especially if the graph is going up and down. Either the goal is too difficult at this point or the method of teaching is ineffective and needs to be changed. Every IEP should have changes of one sort or the other. If your child is not progressing, something needs to change. Period.

Hire an Advocate

If your research has hit a wall, your child has not been diagnosed as you believe he or she should be, or you in any way feel something is wrong, it's time to enlist an advocate. In some regions, they are available without a fee but not all. Use a local autism resource to locate an advocate. When you do, meet with them—even if via phone—and ask them plenty of questions to make sure they're a good fit. Enlist them to come to your IEP.

Advocates can be amazing helpers. Just their presence in the room can change the entire dynamic of a meeting. But remember that they are still somewhat beholden to the school system as well as biases that may exist in the education system itself. Choose one wisely and get to know them well. A good advocate can stand alongside your child for his or her entire education. We are very blessed that our county provides one.

Even if you cannot locate one, I advise you never attend your child's IEP meeting alone. Having an informed professional in your corner will help when things get rocky or contentious.

Know the School's Limitations

School budget cuts are a reality today. There is only so much a teacher can do when aides and paraprofessionals are limited, class sizes are out of control, and teacher turnover is high. Some teachers have been asked to do things that no human being can possibly achieve, sometimes for extremely low pay, and frankly, I'm surprised that more of them haven't quit. (This goes to show the depth of passion most teachers have for building the minds and character of our kids.)

Please be sympathetic to this. Educate yourself on where your school lies in the spectrum of public education. You may be asking for the impossible, so stick to what you honestly think can be improved when making requests.

Be Involved to Learn about Problems

Yea, I know, it's hard to ask parents of kids with disabilities to get more involved. Between paperwork, doctor appointments, therapy, alternative care, support programs, medicines/supplements, special diets, money, work, and more, how on earth can you be more involved? Sometimes, though, this gig of parenting doesn't just call for hard choices, it calls for impossible ones. Remember that with God, nothing is impossible.

You need to balance everything in your life versus what is best for your child, and that includes his or her future. It's not going to be easy, but if you are not involved in either the school or the school board, it will be much harder to effectively advocate for your child. And the truth is that no matter how top-flight your advocate is, the *best* advocate for your child is *you*. Prayerfully, review your work schedule and seriously consider ways in which you can find time to be more involved. Learn whom you can trust — or not trust. Seek the Lord's help in guiding you on what to do next and how.

Figure Out How to Achieve Your Goals for Your Child

You have goals for your child. It may be that she will have a job one day, or go to college, or he may live in a group home, or she may just need to learn how to keep herself safe. Depending on your child's abilities and limitations, you may not know what will happen in adulthood, but you do have some grasp of where he or she can land in one, two, or five years. Take those and run with them! What great thing did the teacher say about your kid that you'd like to be built upon? What's gnawing at you that didn't work?

For example, my older daughter is not good at Spanish and doesn't like it, and I honestly don't think she has a clue what it's all about. She was better off spending that time mastering her first language or learning about Spanish culture. I called an IEP meeting, and we made the change, which is more practical for her. She had a smoother school experience after that.

If you are an involved parent, the teachers and staff will know and respect this and be more open to suggestions, especially if they make sense within the structure of the school. Remember, they also want your child to have a smoother experience to make their job easier.

Advocate for Inclusion

I advocate for inclusion, which is an adaptation of the Least Restricted Environment (LRE) that your child can learn in. As a parent, how much inclusion your child has should be your choice. Research shows that students with disabilities do better when fully included as much as possible. The ideal is for your child to study the same subjects at the same time as other kids, in the same room, with an aide if needed, at the level of their IEP.

Don't say, "I'm good with a life skills class," if that's not what you feel is best. It's your job to advocate, which is especially true if your child has autism but is not academically successful. How can he or she learn appropriate behaviors if he or she is not included with kids who know how to behave appropriately? (This is one of my pet peeves with segregated "autistic support" classrooms.)

Inclusion has also been shown to be beneficial to *other* children. I'm passionate about this after my people-loving oldest child (who does not have autism) was segregated into autistic support in kindergarten because they didn't know what else to do with her. She was put in a class with two other students who did not speak or socialize. She was only included for about five minutes a day in kindergarten, during which time she was fed Skittles. Our neighbor's son, who was in her class, had no idea the following year who she was or that she was even in his grade.

Your child should be included as much as he or she can for the good of the whole community. This will take work, lots of it, and support, but it will prepare your child to be a functional member of society when he or she grows up. You can have more or less inclusion, depending on the school. As mentioned, our middle school frowned upon it, and high school is a whole different experience! While my high schooler has some inclusive activities, most of the time she is in autistic support. The flipside of inclusion is that kids with special needs are more likely to associate with their peers who also have special needs, which is also beneficial. Weigh this issue carefully.

Prepping for the Meeting

A few weeks before the meeting, review the IEP draft and make changes or recommendations you'd like for your child. After the first evaluation by your school, you can do regular re-evaluations. Our team normally does them every year, but you can request them as often as you like. You may want to do a re-evaluation before the next IEP timeframe often if your child has made sudden gains intellectually, behaviorally, or socially.

If you have other requests that you'd like to implement, write them down and email it to your teacher a week before the meeting. Discuss them with your advocate or lawyer first.

Be sure to prepare yourself for the day of the meeting. If you arrive expecting a contentious meeting, out of breath, angry, or anxious, with little sleep and no breakfast, you've already set the tableau for how it's going to go.

Stop expecting the worst before you even get out of the car. This can lead to anger, and anger is not your friend during an IEP meeting. Proverbs 29:11 says, "Fools give full vent to their rage, but the wise bring calm in the end." If you feel frustrated and amped up during the meeting, take a water or bathroom break, and say a prayer. I recommend bringing a calming blend of essential oils in a roller or an inhaler to soothe you.

Do your best to come to the IEP at full capacity and try to get a good night's sleep the night before. Pray and read scripture before you arrive to center yourself. Eat something healthy beforehand. If you are frazzled, the staff will take one look at you and be on the offensive.

Be sure to be prepared with the details as soon as possible: Gas the car, organize your questions, notes, and documents, and wear clothes that make you feel confident. If you have an advocate, make sure he or she is on their way if running late.

Know When to School is Not a Good Fit Anymore

Maybe each and every time you go to an IEP meeting, there's a voice inside telling you this will never, ever work for your child. Maybe the staff has *nothing* good to say about your child, and they struggle to write down just one "strength" on your child's IEP. When that happens, it's time to rethink the situation. Maybe your child will be served better by a different school.

As mentioned, the options for educating a child with special needs are greater and more diverse than ever. You can find a temporary solution until something better comes in. I have a friend who has one child with Down syndrome and another gifted child, who both struggled after they relocated. They were not served well at all by the school system, and the family chose to homeschool for one year, while other options were explored for the following year. A difficult but temporary measure, this decision is not for everyone, but you need to honestly lay your cards on the table and figure out what is best for your child's future.

Whatever you choose to do, make sure that God is leading you. You will need His guidance and wisdom to change from what is simple to a more complex option. That includes doing all your due diligence!

I hope these suggestions help you. Remember that the bottom line is not your pride, feelings, or anger. It's not about you at all. It's about making sure that the thirty or so hours a week your child spends in school serves him or her well and opens opportunities, like a career, friendship, and maybe even college or vocational training. Nothing else is at stake. Check your feelings at the door, stride in with confidence, and do the best you can to advocate for your precious child.

Chapter 14

Safeguarding Your Child

The Lord says, "I will rescue those who love Me.
I will protect those who trust in My Name.
When they call on Me, I will answer;
I will be with them in trouble.
I will rescue and honor them.
I will reward them with a long life
and give them My salvation." — Psalm 91: 14-16, NLT

Imagine waking up the last day of your dream Disney vacation to discover that your three-year-old daughter is missing. It's terrifying. I should know because it happened to us.

After seven days of theme park visits, my husband and I put the girls to bed, then crawled into our bed on a Saturday night, exhausted. We had nothing left to do but pack and fly home. We got out of bed on Sunday morning, and as I went to organize the kids for breakfast, I didn't see Zoe. I figured she was hiding in a closet or cabinet as she often did.

But after a few minutes of searching our two-bedroom rental, we realized she was gone. In a moment, we were on the phone to security, the hotel leadership, and the police as we opened every door — kitchen cabinets included — and searched nearby grounds.

When it was apparent that Zoe was missing, my heart leapt into my throat. We were in a resort with *three* swimming pools. I got dizzy thinking about what could happen to my child who did not yet know how to swim.

You might be thinking that what happened was negligence on our part. It wasn't. By the time Zoe was three, she was an expert at getting out of our home. We did everything we could in our home: kept up the baby guard doors, alarms on our doors and windows, double sided locks, etc.

And because we like to travel a lot, we produced makeshift solutions for travel. In a hotel, we merely needed to put something cumbersome like a chair and some kind of noisy item in front of the door. But in a four-room resort, we had to get more creative. For our resort, we blocked the door with the dining room table, thinking she could not get out.

To this day, we don't know how she managed to escape our room.

At this point, I lost the ability to think clearly. It felt like I was in a dream. My mind kept saying, "This isn't happening, is it?" All I saw in my head were images of me walking toward a pool, terrified of what I'd find. Luckily, my brain stopped the scene before I got there.

Not knowing if she was dead or alive was the worst part of that experience.

Soon, the police arrived. The security team from the rental home had already been there, speaking Spanish too rapidly for me to understand. I felt like they were taking *forever*. I kept interrupting and asking them why they weren't out looking, why they weren't checking pools, why they were just standing there?!

It turned out there was a reason. Security had found my daughter hours before, but even when we called them, desperate and terrified, they did not *tell* us they had her. I won't get into all the ugly details, but it did get ugly, which increased our pain.

Seeing my daughter whole and absolutely fine, clueless of the storm around her, was hands down the best moment of my whole life.

This was our first—and thankfully, last—experience with elopement, also called autism wandering.

The Danger of Elopement for Autistic Children

Losing a child thanks to elopement, unfortunately, is common. On March 21, 2017, WebMD posted an article, "Autism Greatly Boosts Risk of Drowning."[1] A study revealed that kids on the spectrum are a whopping *160 times more* likely to drown than their non-autistic peers, and often, autistic children who go missing are found drowned.

That's frightening, but I can't say I'm surprised. Non-autistic kids often drown because they are left unattended at pool parties. But children on the autism spectrum often lack awareness of danger. If they get away from home unsupervised, they are often attracted to water and may enter even if they don't know how to swim.

It doesn't matter what time of year it is, either, or if you are home. Years back, an autistic child went missing from a New Year's Eve party hosted by the parents. The child's body was discovered in a creek a few days later. As in most of these cases, people blamed the parents. It was not, however, their fault.

Elopement happens fast, and you may not be aware of it. It can happen when you are sleeping, in the shower, or on the toilet. It can happen if you run in the basement to check out a leak, get deep into cleaning, or are looking for something lost in your closet. It can happen if you are hosting a party to ensure the environment is safe for your child or you have a fenced-off backyard with a door the child can open or climb under. It can easily happen in crowded venues like theme parks or shopping malls.

1.   https://www.webmd.com/brain/autism/features/autism-elopement-wandering

When autistic kids get lost, they are exposed to dangers they might not understand. They may not be able to ask for help. And since kids on the autism spectrum have a lower regard for danger, they are under greater risk than other children.

According to the AWAARE Collaboration, a division of the National Autism Association that helps prevent elopement, about half of all kids with autism engage in wandering.

Unfortunately, parents are often blamed, even when circumstances are beyond their control. My daughter's case of elopement in Florida landed us a call from Child Protective Services in Pennsylvania. The case was closed as quickly as it was opened, but that didn't make it any less stressful.

And for those of you who think I might be at fault, I want you to know that Zoe was asleep in a bed with her older sister, in a room with her grandmother, behind a locked front door whose bolts we thought she could not reach, with heavy furniture blocking it off.

She was determined to leave. That family in Pennsylvania who lost their child on New Year's Eve? They took heat because they hosted a party. I've done that: host a party so I could be sure my child is around and won't get lost in a stranger's house. I'm 100 percent sure they thought their child was safe.

But even that can fail.

How to Protect Your Child from Wandering

What can you do to prevent your child from wandering when you are asleep, away, or otherwise engaged? You have to protect your child while still being able to go on with your life, if only just so you can go to the bathroom or shower once in a blue moon.

Here are options available to you, many of which we have used.

Install a security system in your home. Initially, we considered installing an alarm for security purposes when we moved into our home. But when the technician told us that it could be programmed to alert you when a door or window is opened, we said, "We'll take it!" When you open a door or a first-floor window, a robotic voice tells you exactly which one is open: "living room window." It's extremely helpful to keep track of open doors and windows.

Put up flip locks. At one point, Zoe kept going in the basement, which is where we keep the water heater, Wi-Fi router, and Christmas tree. One winter, she turned off the water heater on a frosty day. We didn't realize it for hours. That's when we installed flip locks, which prevented her from opening that door and were a challenge to her for many years. (They can even be difficult for tired adults!) Your child will figure them out sooner or later, but they work well for younger children.

Use a baby gate. We kept a baby gate on Zoe's bedroom door for years, until she was too old for it to block her. Our bedroom is nearby, so we could always hear her call, but the gate stopped her from getting up before us and leaving by the front or back door when she was little. We put toys in her room, so in the mornings, she'd play contentedly until we got up. Eventually, she outgrew it, but it helped us keep her safe when she was at the most risk.

Build a fence if you have a yard. In 2007, we bought a house specifically because it had a big backyard. But once my daughter was diagnosed with autism, we stopped using the yard due to our fears, until we built a six-foot-high fence. It was costly (around $10,000) and required that we put a double lock on the gate to prevent her exiting except through the house, but it was worth every penny. On nice days, she could enjoy the yard without worry.

In fact, we applied for an autism waiver that only covered a fraction of the cost but was extremely helpful. Look for resources in your area, or if you are handy, you can build your own fence.

Use a child harness. I used umbrella strollers when we'd go to theme parks until Zoe was too big for them, but you can use a child harness if you — and your child — are good with it. I've seen plenty of kids wearing them at Disney World so there's no shame in using one in such crowded areas.

Teach your child to swim. I wanted to give Zoe professional swimming lessons like I did for my older daughter, but she struggled with the attention required for a formal lesson. Fortunately, she taught herself to swim. One year, we were at a resort, and she ran into the pool. While I worried that she was running, she went to a shallow part and started swimming! The running start helped her kick up her feet and after a few attempts, she got the hang of it.

After that, my husband and I made sure we got her to kick up her feet and float as often as possible. Within a year, she could swim like a fish and is amazing at floating. Do yourself this favor and teach your autistic child to swim. You won't regret it!

Get your child a service dog. If you can find a nearby service dog provider, you may want to check this out. It can be costly, but it may be a deductible medical expense. You may also be able to get an autism waiver for this. Note that service dogs have a formal education that specifically helps them save the lives of their humans. Any dog can act as a support dog with minimal training, but an autism service dog requires time and training to truly protect your child from danger.

Block the doors when traveling. When we travel, we block the doors with things like ironing boards and garbage pails in a hotel room, or big furniture in a condo rental. Of course, she can open them but we make sure they are set up to make a loud crashing noise that will wake us if she does! We've also learned to make sure she has plenty to do if she wakes up before us so she won't be tempted to leave, such as access to tech, books, drawing tools, food, and drink. (Keeping her busy or up late the night before to help her sleep in is another tactic!)

Use a GPS tracking device to prevent autism wandering. This is controversial, I'll admit, due to the dangers of EMF (more on that later), which is why we use radiation shields on many of our devices. Some kids wander more than others, and some wander much less when they get older (like my daughter). You can either get a special device for them to wear or download an app on their phone. Additionally, your child may even wear a bracelet or device that attaches to his or her clothing. Do a search on "autism tracking devices" to find all your options.

If your child is old enough to have a phone or other device instead of a standard GPS system, make sure that location is always on so you can track him or her. Additionally, you may want to program a safe number so your child can contact you with one button in whatever way they can communicate.

Have an emergency plan. While you should have a standard emergency plan for your family, you should also have an emergency plan for if your child goes missing. This plan should involve friends, neighbors, and loved ones, who can keep an eye out for your child.

NAA provides the Big Red Safety Box, which includes things like two window alarms, a Family Wandering Emergency Plan, ID cards, and more. Learn more. NationalAutismAssociation.org/big-red-safety-box.

You can also enroll your child in Project Lifesaver, which connects you with local authorities, such as the police, to safeguard your child or with a tracking device for a lower cost. Learn more at ProjectLifeSaver.org.

Teach your child safety measures. As much as possible, teach your child what they are cognitively able to understand to stay safe should they get lost. This includes things like:

- What walk signs and stop signs mean
- How to identify helpers by uniform (police, firefighters, doctors)
- How to walk on the sidewalk versus the street
- How to scream and kick up a fuss if they are grabbed
- Water safety

There are no easy solutions for this problem, but there are measures you can take today to give your child the best chance to stay safe.

Always pray for God to protect your child and keep you aware of where your child is at all times.

Chapter 15

Puberty and Sex

She is clothed with strength and dignity,
and she laughs without fear of the future. – Proverbs 31:25, NLT

Now if your child is profoundly disabled, you may be wondering if you even need this chapter. I assure you that you do. The world today is decimating Christian morals on every front, and there is no more embattled topic today than sexuality in our youth.

Before we start, let's get clear about what God wants from us in terms of avoiding sin in sexuality.

God's Design for Sex

If you are a Christian, then sex:

- Is not about two people getting what they want.
- Is not about chemistry, biology, evolution, physicality, attraction, or pheromones. While I love science and while the Lord designed sex within its laws, it is not the driving factor behind sex.
- It's not even about procreation. It's *necessary* to reproduce, but reproduction is not required for marital sex. After all, one day you'll be past child-bearing age.

God designed sex to be a metaphor for His great love for us. This is a bit clearer to see when we look at the Biblical traditions around marriage, which were also designed by God. Couples were betrothed, rather than engaged. This was just as serious a commitment as marriage and as difficult to get out of. The betrothed couple would wait for their wedding and then, when all the rites and celebrations were done, husband and wife come together to consummate the marriage in the ultimate expression of romantic love.

God invites all souls to partake in a "betrothal" with our Savior (also known as salvation) that will last for all of eternity (the "marriage"). This is clearly illustrated by the Bible when Paul calls the church as the bride of Christ (2 Corinthians 11:2; Ephesians 5:24-27). This is also proclaimed in Revelation 19:7 and 21:2.

Jesus refers to Himself as the bridegroom in Mark 2:19-20. John the Baptist also did in John 3:29. Jesus also compares the kingdom of heaven to a wedding feast. (Matthew 22:2 and 25:1) That's salvation.

Sex Belongs Only Between a Husband and a Wife

As we are waiting here for Jesus to return or to bring us home when we die, likewise the betrothed couple in God's design waits for the joy of the wedding before consummation. It's the happy ending we've all been longing for.

As described in chapter 10, this metaphor is partly why God created marriage. That's why sexual immorality is incredibly offensive to Him. It's not just a sin and a violation of His commandments. It's a direct smear to the holy example of the relationship between the Son and His bride, the church.

The Bible tells us to flee sexual sins over and over, but I think it's most clear in Paul's letter to the church in Corinthians:

> The body is not meant for sexual immorality, but for the Lord, and the Lord for the body. And God raised the Lord and will also raise us up by His power. Do you not know that your bodies are members of Christ? Shall I then take the members of Christ and make them members of a prostitute? Never! Or do you not know that he who is joined to a prostitute becomes one body with her? For, as it is written, "The two will become one flesh." But he who is joined to the Lord becomes one spirit with Him. Flee from sexual immorality. Every other sin a person commits is outside the body, but the sexually immoral person sins against his own body. Or do you not know that your body is a temple of the Holy Spirit within you, whom you have from God? You are not your own, for you were bought with a price. So glorify God in your body. — 1 Corinthians. 6:13b-20, ESV

Sleeping around outside of marriage violates that and is a sin. And that separates us from God in the same way cheating on your spouse separates you from your husband.

Why You Must Teach Your Children about Sex

Now you may be thinking, "I didn't wait! How do I talk to my kids about sex when I didn't?" Well, that's okay. Let me share my perspective.

Do I wish I waited? I do. In my youth, I worried that it would go horribly wrong if I waited for my wedding night and I'd end up divorced. I had no clue about sex on any level, much less spiritually, since I was not a Christian at the time. My mother came from an older generation that did not talk about sex — or menstruation, childbirth, or any other personal female matter either.

And so, I had nothing to go on except the whispers of friends and relatives and books that were inappropriate for my age.

I wish my mom had taught me what purity and waiting is all about, even if I didn't understand it well. I wish I could have seen sex as a wonderful union, a promise, a blessing, and a deepening of commitment. I wish I had an idea what the waiting was all about, what the devotion, commitment, and love signified, what the connection truly meant, rather than just the "you must wait or else!" Nothing will get a teen to violate your wishes faster than telling him or her they can't do something.

The world taught me weird and conflicting things about sex: That it's about lust and desire, that it's messy, that it's fun and wild, that it's hard to imagine, that it's supposed to be dirty, that it needs to happen before marriage. The list of incorrect and confusing information I got on this topic torpedoed any chance I had at having a healthy sexual relationship, much less a Godly one.

Your children will one day want to learn about sex. Even autistic kids will feel the impact of hormones on their body and need to know how to handle that. Some disabled people may not be interested until they are older but eventually, they will probably want to know.

Disabled people are also one of the highest victim groups of sexual crimes, so you need to teach your children the truth to give them the best chance to be aware and stay safe. And if you have not laid a Biblical foundation for them, they will get 100 percent of their information from the culture's shifting morality and that is not a good place to be!

This, then, is what I needed to teach my children: sex, virginity, and waiting for a spouse who loves you are God's ideal design in these matters. They don't have to be privy to the intimate details of our sex life, but they can see the fruits of that practice in our marriage or relationships with the opposite sex. To teach them about sex really means teaching them about God's design for marriage and the more difficult parts of marriage: tough love, sacrifice, commitment, and serving your spouse. In twenty-five years of marriage, that's what I've learned!

Don't Give in to Defeatist Parenting

I was once talking with a friend who said, "I got those condoms at my daughter's high school. They have a bowl of them in the nurse's room." I must have had a funny look on my face because she immediately followed this up with, "I agree with them giving them out! She's just going to do it anyway. Better safe than sorry."

My heart broke when I heard that. She had taught her daughter, by her words and by openly gleeful reaction to the condoms, that there was no other option than to have sex before marriage.

The discussion stayed with me for a long time, as I mulled over the things I knew and believed. That day I changed from "engaged mom" to "engaged *Christian* mom" in the area of teaching about sex. I absolutely refused to be defeated ("she's going to do it anyway") by the culture and my own past before I even started.

Here what I came to realize:

- For those of us who were sexually active before marriage, there is a tendency to shy away from teaching your children purity because you feel like a hypocrite. You don't want your child to make the same mistakes you did, but you do want them to have a healthy sex life. You don't want to share the intimate details of ungodly sexual choices, but you want to be honest. The reality is that was your past. As a Christian, the Lord has forgiven all your sins, including premarital sex. You are a new creation and as such, fully equipped to teach your kids from your new perspective.

- For new Christian parents, this may pose additional problems. Perhaps in the past you've said that extramarital sex is fine, as long as your partner is not married and "justified" (i.e., you're in love). Besides, you did, and you turned out fine, right? Let her live her life. Or you don't really see your past actions as sins yet. But the same thing applies to you as well. You are a new creation, with a new set of beliefs, so you must set aside the person you were before and give your child correct and "updated" information from the new you.

- For more mature Christians, your mind is made up and you want to teach the Godly approach to sex, but you are uncertain how to do that. What do you say about a past that didn't leave you sexually scarred because God had already forgave your past sins? You may feel your lack of experience could push away your child, but you, too, are perfectly equipped to help your child learn about this sensitive topic.

- I feel like I've been through each and every stage of this, but now I came out on the right side of what I should be saying and doing to help my children understand what they need to look out for in these matters.

The Problem with "She or He Will Do It Anyway"

Before starting, I wanted to address this mindset. I realize that we live in a scary, challenging world. It's pulling your child from every direction, and in fact, they are getting terribly mixed messages: "Wear plunging necklines" versus "Breastfeeding in public is disgusting." "Don't overindulge or drink and drive" versus "nothing that happens to you while you're passed out drunk/high is your fault." "Look sexy and provocative and flaunt it!" versus "Men are pigs for lusting after women."

And here's another: "I want my daughter to be safe, secure, and empowered" versus "When it comes to sex, she'll do whatever."

I am not telling you to avoid teaching your child about birth control and sex. My mother left this out as she was raising me, and it hurt me in many ways. I made really poor and stupid choices. God must have been watching over me because I made it out of my youth with no physical consequences, although with an unhealthy attitude about sex. Please teach your child about sex and birth control. It's an important responsibility.

But before you do that, you must teach your child your values. For those of you who are on the fence with this topic, I want you to go back in time and imagine your mother tossing condoms at you, saying, "Well, I know you're going to have sex anyway, so here." And maybe she did do that. The question is, how did that make you feel?

What we say is not necessarily what our children actually hear. I know if my mom had said that to me, I'd have felt like she just gave up on me. I can imagine kids — boys and girls — thinking any of these things:

- "Well, then I can do anything I want."
- "Cool, no rules for me."
- "As long as I have a condom, I'm protected all the time from everything."
- "So then it's true. I have to have sex to get anyone to like me. Even Mom agrees."
- "Sex is part of growing up."

You may even be thinking, "My kid knows better." And I hope he or she does. Bring your brain back to when you were a teenager. We all had immature thought patterns, mixed up with hopped-up hormones. And a lot of us misinterpreted anything our parents said. Teenaged minds are experts at twisting anything to support either their own desires or their distorted view of themselves, sometimes both at the same time.

Setting up your teenage children with birth control is defeatist parenting, in my opinion. You are telling your child that you have zero impact on his or her actions at this age so you're just giving up.

Now it's a different issue if you think that your child will never be intimate, and you are trying to protect them. Many parents with special needs children consider permanent birth control like an IUD or other surgeries. We are a holistic family, so that is not an option for us. I believe that any type of foreign device in or surgery on your child's body can have adverse events or unforeseen consequences. But this is your decision to make along with Jesus. Whatever you decide, please do not make this decision out of fear. Instead, pray deeply on the matter and do a great deal of research on your options and what can happen. Weigh all risks and benefits.

Conquering Defeatist Parenting

No matter how old your children are, or what challenges they face, it is time to educate them about sex and what God requires as best as you can to protect them from any future harm.

Let's conquer defeatist and fearful parenting by walking hand in hand with the Lord to teach our children Godly sexual values. Here are things to remember:

Kids Are Listening to Us

We've been told that kids don't listen to their parents, but that's just not true. They do listen and value your words. Even if they rebel a bit, most eventually come back to the wisdom you taught them.

As a Christian, my wisdom comes from the Holy Spirit and Scripture. And I can only teach what I know, understand, and believe. Do I make mistakes? I sure do, but I try to acknowledge that and correct it when God tells me. I even apologize to my kids when I'm wrong. I am grateful that I have given them the basic tools to learn about their bodies to help safeguard them against inappropriate advances.

Don't Fool Yourself

While it's fine to believe that right precautionary tools can protect your child from the consequences of sex, there is still significant risk associated with it. Condoms break, birth control pills can be missed, IUDs fail, and the HPV vaccine* wasn't made for every sexually transmitted type of HPV, much less other STDs. And that doesn't even cover the poor choices a growing mind can make, particularly if they are under the influence of drugs, alcohol, or that old teenager enemy, peer pressure. Be honest about your child's risk in these areas.

Fix Yourself First

Before you talk with your children about sex, first you need to get right with God yourself. As a Christian, you need to confront your past. If you sinned before you came to faith, or even after, the Holy Spirit can and will correct your wrong thinking.

Yes, I said "wrong thinking." For years after becoming a Christian, I struggled with my premarital sexual past with my husband. I always looked at what, when, and how we did what we did from a non-Christian and, frankly, feminist worldview. It can be a hard myth for Christian women to break, but God broke it in me. Only He can change your mindset on sex. In fact, He did this for me on two of the most contentious issues today: abortion and homosexuality.

Now I know that things I did and thought were sins by God's standards, but I also don't have excess guilt about the things I didn't understand were wrong at the time. I confessed, God forgave me, and I moved on. The Lord will do all this work in your heart if you let Him.

How to Talk Honestly

You may be thinking, "But I had sex before marriage. Am I supposed to lie to my kids?"

Hold up, there. First of all, you and your husband keep your sex life private from your kids, right? How is this any different? You don't have to confess to your children your sexual sins, but you can choose to select key turning points, truths learned, or any overarching "wrong thinking" you had.

---

*I do not endorse this vaccine, nor any other, and I encourage parents to do their own research on the effectiveness and safety of vaccines, over and above what doctors and government agencies tell you.

Secondly, this is a good opportunity to teach your kids the fact that human values are not necessarily God's values. Just because a thing "feels" right doesn't mean it is. Christian kids need to know that only God can teach them right from wrong, first through their parents, then through other Christians, Scripture, trials, and so on.

We all make mistakes. I hate to break it to you, but your kids already know you mess up plenty. Recently, Amelia told me off for saying a bad word — respectfully, I might add. I can't fault her for that. If you think you can't admit your mistakes to your kids, think again. They already know you're a sinner. For example, Amelia is quick to point out anytime either of us says a "bad word."

Remember that the Bible tasks us with teaching our kids about Jesus and how to be more Christ-like, but only God can make it happen. And that's the truth. God *can* make that happen. The world says that people can't change, but the gospel tells us that God replaces hearts of stone with hearts of flesh. We all start out with this sin naturally, but hearts can and do change, when Jesus comes into your life and still more as you grow in Him.

You can use your failures to highlight how and why God gifted humans with sex because it is a gift but only when it is done in accordance with God's will. Sex outside of the Lord's standards always has consequences, even if they are not tangible. You can teach your children, too, how to move forward on the right track, even if they have started off on the wrong foot.

Four Keys to Teaching Your Autistic Child about Sex

I know this seems like a daunting job, but it is required of you. You can do this properly. These tips come from my own experience in raising daughters. (Note: If you are married to a Christian man, it is better to have your husband teach your sons.)

I've set out several tasks in order, challenges you might face in doing so, and scriptures that you can refer to.

Task: Teaching Self-Respect

Your first task is to teach them self-respect. Let them know that their body is a gift from God and is beautiful, even with all its flaws. Compliment their strengths, from physical to social to their personality and have them thank God for these blessings. Jesus made us and loves us exactly as we are.

Challenges: Your own struggles with body image, looks, and vanity and self-deprecating comments, such as, "I hate my belly," can make this difficult for you.

Scripture:

How we were created:

- Psalm 139, which dives deep into how well the Lord knows, and how we are wonderfully and fearfully made. The book *Audrey Bunny* by Angie Smith is a beautiful children's book based around Psalm

139:14 that I highly recommend. It's written for ages four to eight. My daughters both absolutely loved this book, and they are usually not interested in books. This book teaches God has a special place in His heart for those the world calls "lowly." Those of us who are adopted by the Lord are given all that we need when we surrender to Him, to be powerful, wise, and strong so that we might boast in Him and not ourselves.

- Wisdom: consider your calling, brothers: not many of you were wise according to worldly standards, not many were powerful, not many were of noble birth. But God chose what is foolish in the world to shame the wise; God chose what is weak in the world to shame the strong; God chose what is low and despised in the world, even things that are not, to bring to nothing things that are, so that no human being might boast in the presence of God. — 1 Corinthians 1:26-29
- Body image: To help your child achieve a positive body image, you can share this verse. This is when the Lord instructed the prophet Samuel to choose David, the youngest of many brothers and just a lowly sheepherder for the king. David is known as the greatest king of Israel and a man after God's own heart:

But the Lord said to Samuel, "Do not look on his appearance or on the height of his stature, because I have rejected him. For the Lord sees not as man sees: man looks on the outward appearance, but the Lord looks on the heart." —1 Samuel 16:7, ESV

- For girls, you can also teach the book of Esther, which is about a woman who saved the remnant of the Jewish nation. I recommend finding a good children's book on this subject.

Task: Teach Body Functions

This is an excellent opportunity to teach the creation story. It's also a good opportunity to review that we were made in God's image. This is something I seeded into Amelia and Zoe for many years.

One important note: I'm a firm believer in teaching kids the appropriate names for body parts and sexual organs. One time, we hired a childcare provider who said to me, "Why don't you just save 'down there' instead of vagina?" She thought it was wrong to teach them the appropriate terms, but I responded, "Because if she's in pain, how will I know where?" Being embarrassed about proper medical terminology is an issue of shame, and that may require the Lord's healing.

Challenges: You may struggle if you do not take the creation story literally. That's okay, though. It's in the Bible and can be still useful for teaching even if your children are at a lower intellectual level. If they are of a higher level, you can teach it as a metaphor.

Other challenges include:

- Menstruation training and preparation for girls: If your daughter is not yet menstruating but the time is approaching, start buying sanitary pads and teach her to wear them. Talk to her about her monthly cycle that is coming and that there will be bleeding, but it's not an injury. Let her try to wear the pads now before she needs them.
- Issues such as masturbation and other puberty challenges for children of both sexes: I'll admit this is a challenging topic, but these are some natural issues that every teen will deal with. I advise you to seek advice from older moms in your church or a pastor who you can speak freely with.

Scripture:
We were created by God and in His image:

- Know that the Lord is God. It is He who made us, and we are His; we are His people, the sheep of his pasture. – Psalm 100:3, NIV
- Then God said, "Let Us make man in Our image, after Our likeness. And let them have dominion over the fish of the sea and over the birds of the heavens and over the livestock and over all the earth and over every creeping thing that creeps on the earth." — Genesis 1:26, ESV
- Teach your child the creation story in Genesis 1. It's a good idea to go through the entire text, perhaps a day of creation for each day of the week. Again, there are numerous children's books centered around this scripture.

We were created for a purpose:

- For we are His workmanship, created in Christ Jesus for good works, which God prepared beforehand, that we should walk in them. — Ephesians 2:10, ESV
- Now the word of the Lord came to me, saying, "Before I formed you in the womb I knew you, and before you were born I consecrated you I appointed you a prophet to the nations." — Jeremiah 1:4-5, ESV
- "For I know the plans I have for you," declares the Lord, "plans to prosper you and not to harm you, plans to give you hope and a future." — Jeremiah 29:11, NIV

Task: Teaching Privacy and Safety

Many kids with disabilities struggle with these issues, and people on the autism spectrum often struggle with safety because they sometimes do not have a well-formed concept of fear. The emotion of fear is what teaches us to be safe.

You must teach your children "this is private, no one sees this except Mom, Dad, and the doctor."

Challenges: Make the distinction between appropriate and inappropriate touching, and shift to hugging/kissing less, especially if you are an affectionate family. Sensory issues or a child in diapers or who needs help with toileting, especially at an older age, can be more challenging.

Teach your child to contrast between purposeful nudity (showering, doctor visits) and the use of nudity in sexuality. I will admit that despite my best efforts, some of this has been a challenge for my kids to keep in their mind but still, do your best. Over time, they have learned better habits so you may need a lot of patience.

Scripture:

Privacy:

- And on those parts of the body that we think less honorable we bestow the greater honor, and our unpresentable parts are treated with greater modesty. — 1 Corinthians 12:23, ESV

Safety:

- This scripture is really for you. We do our best to teach our children safety, but ultimately, we must trust the Lord to protect our children when they cannot grasp safety issues.
- Have I not commanded you? Be strong and courageous. Do not be frightened, and do not be dismayed, for the Lord your God is with you wherever you go. — Joshua 1:9, ESV

Task: Teaching about the Opposite Sex, Love, and Marriage

Teach your children where babies come from and how they are made in love by sharing with them how they were made. Or, if you or someone you know is pregnant, you can use that as a wonderful opportunity to teach them as well.

Challenge: Determine when and if your autistic child will have sexual impulses, date, or marry. Boundaries are also challenging to create if your kids do not bring home friends or are friends with members of the opposite sex.

Another challenge is having them meet other kids with disabilities on their level. All you can do is plan.

Scripture:
Marriage:

- Genesis 2:18-24 shares God's design for marriage, including how the two become one. I advise you to study this first, particularly if you have had a challenging time with marriage.

Sex:

- Song of Solomon is a love song that explicitly describes how sex in marriage should be, including the expectation for people who are engaged. It is extremely poetic, so it can be a challenge to read.

- A great resource is the book, *7 Biblical Lessons to Make Sense of Puberty* by Luke Gilkerson. It's written for ages four to eight, so it could be a good fit, depending on your child's intellectual level. It was helpful for Amelia and Zoe. They were fully engaged and even colored in some of the pictures. There are explicit and accurate images. Each chapter is based on scripture, covering all kinds of topics, from the development of a fetus to rape. There are more books in this series for older age groups, if your child can read text-only books.

Healing Resources for Adults

Now if you yourself are struggling with sex and discovering how it can be pure, I also have some grown up recommendations:

- *The Good Girl's Guide to Great Sex: (and You Thought Bad Girls Have All the Fun)* by Sheila Wray Gregoire covers all, and I mean all, the questions an adult woman is afraid to ask about Biblical sex.
- If any Christian woman out there is troubled by *50 Shades of Gray*, or thinks it's "okay" as a guilty pleasure, please read *Pulling Back the Shades: Erotica, Intimacy, and the Longings of a Woman's Heart* by Dr. Juli Slattery and Dannah Gresh.

Your Child's Values about Sex Rely on You

Here's the thing. Satan totally wants you to have a defeatist attitude. He is counting on you to say "better safe than sorry" and avoid the hard discussions with your child, and by hard, I mean not just sex, but also rape, date rape, porn, abortion, sanctity of life, etc. Your job is to teach your child Godly values. It's not easy. It's frightening and challenging, but it's your duty.

If you don't teach your child what's right, the world will quickly and convincingly step in and teach him or her the wrong way to wisdom. That is exactly what happened to me, and it caused untold sin and pain. (No, I'm not blaming my mom. I was a smart kid, but I used it to pursue the world's truth.) This is true if you have a boy or a girl, if your child is disabled or gifted or neither, if your child can talk wisely or not speak at all.

Chapter 16

Helping Your Child Pursue God's Plan for His or Her Purpose

Now may the God of peace who brought again from the dead our Lord Jesus, the great shepherd of the sheep, by the blood of the eternal covenant, equip you with everything good that you may do his will, working in us that which is pleasing in his sight, through Jesus Christ, to whom be the glory forever and ever. Amen. – Hebrews 13:20-21, ESV
For we are God's masterpiece. He has created us anew in Christ Jesus, so we can do the good things he planned for us long ago. – Ephesians 2:10, NLT

Your child has a God-given purpose on this Earth. God designed each and every creature on this planet with a purpose, but humans are, as the scripture says, His "masterpiece."

When you have a child with a severe developmental disability who is on the autism spectrum, it can be difficult to see that purpose. I have two children. As I've mentioned, my oldest, Amelia, has Down syndrome. While she has some ADHD issues and sensory problems, as well as numerous developmental disabilities, I always knew her purpose in life. Her cheerful good nature helped me out of my postpartum depression. Her resilience influences and changes me. Her caring ability and nurturing attitude make it easy for her to make friends, despite her speech limitations. She has a heart for encouragement and is a blessing to everyone she meets.

Zoe, however, struggles with all of those things. That's partly due to many of the challenges that are common for kids on the autism spectrum, such as sensory problems, behavior, communication, etc. It took time and healing for me to get my first glimpse of the beautiful person who lies beneath her challenges. She cried so much as a baby that I had to hold her all the time. She can be temperamental or even aggressive when she is sick, in pain, or just plain doesn't get her way.

But God has taught me so much through her as well. In fact, I'd say that I have far more in common with Zoe than Amelia. I understand being overly sensitive, deeply emotional, and misunderstood by even those closest to me. I've held her in my arms when the tears wouldn't stop, when her biggest request in the whole world was for me to tell her it was okay, even though I had no idea why she was crying.

I can see why God placed each of my children in my life, and therefore, I know that it is my duty to help nurture them into a purposeful future.

How do you do this? It's a bit of give and take. There are things your child will be able to do, with God's enablement or healing, that you cannot imagine right now. However, there may be things that your child will never be able to do. Don't tie your hope into a specific dream that you have for them.

Instead, consider that even if your child did not have autism, you still would not be able to build their dreams or create their future life for them. But for children with severe limitations in social, behavioral, and other difficulties, parents need to be a bit more hands on in creating a future that fits for them.

Letting Go of Unrealistic Goals

The world tells us that all people on the autism spectrum are incredibly gifted or intelligent. Maybe your child is, maybe your child isn't, and maybe your child was and is no more. Or maybe your child is very intelligent but not in a way that allows him or her to share or use their knowledge.

God's purpose, though, is bigger: His purpose always brings Him glory and testifies to others about His great love. As I've taught my kids, the life of a follower of Jesus centers on "love God, love people."

Meet your child where he or she is now. Although protocols and therapies may help them overall, you need to help them thrive where they are today. Don't give up hope that God can work an amazing miracle in their lives, but don't hold on to something that you have no guarantee will ever happen.

And this is a back and forth too. For example, I always have hope that non-lethal medical issues can and indeed will be healed in God's time. For example, gut challenges that cause behaviors can be cured. However, it might take years of trying different things to find the right solution.

How can you plan for their futures? Here are a few simple tips:

- **Pray for their future careers.** Ask God to put in your heart what He thinks they should be doing. Pray for revelations and for eyes to see what they can do.
- **Look at all your options.** It's never too soon to start thinking about and researching vocational schools, high school special education programs, colleges that support autistic people, online colleges, programs that provide job coaching/vocational support, etc. Some of these options are very costly or have long waiting lists so you want to be aware of them as soon as possible in order to make plans.
- **What do they like to do?** Of course, this seems obvious, but start looking at general issues as well as tasks while keeping a career in mind. Is your child good with fine motor tasks? Do they prefer to avoid people? Are they good with numbers? Do they excel at something simple but useful, like folding clothes? All those things

can play a role in what their future may look like. Zoe, for example, not only loves music, she also loves to sync up cartoons with her own soundtrack, and she's pretty good at it too!

- **Consider their strengths.** What do teachers and other support personnel say about your child's strengths? You might be surprised if they excel at a task like sewing or other activities that can translate into a job.
- **Think outside the box.** My daughter loves food and food toys, so I'm trying to see if something in the culinary field could work for her. What does your child love to do?

Finding Purpose by Exploring the World

As your child grows, you'll be able to see more opportunities and possibilities. Please don't pass them by! I know that it's easier to stay home and avoid taking your child out, but you need to expose your child to life, people, and community. That will help you find things they like.

The way to get started is by indulging them in their interests. A kid who likes Thomas the Tank Engine should be allowed to explore all kinds of opportunities with trains, from rides to exhibits to journeys. As I mentioned, Zoe's love of music and video has led to some exciting possibilities for her future. Does your child like history, art, photography, music, or animals? Look for opportunities to engage your child.

Here are several options to get your child involved in community beyond school. Look for:

- Local **Special Olympics events**, which features numerous sports options for people under the age of twenty-one.
- **Miracle League** baseball team, where everyone gets a turn at bat. This sport has been great for building my kids' self-esteem!
- US Youth Soccer **TOPSoccer**, which provides opportunities for kids with disabilities to play soccer.
- **Martial arts** organizations that focus on training children provide special training for kids with special needs.
- **Local organizations, daycare centers, gyms, dance, and gymnastic schools, etc.,** that feature sports for kids with disabilities, such as dance schools or gymnastic centers.
- **Tim Tebow's Night to Shine** is an event hosted by local churches every February. It's sort of like prom for young people with special needs.
- Many times, **horse farms** will offer special needs services, including hippotherapy/equine assisted therapy, riding lessons, and more.

You should also look for local resources that can help your child find sensory-friendly or autism-friendly events like plays, movies, and other types of performances. There are also organizations that get children and teens on the autism spectrum involved with theater activities, both onstage and behind the scenes. Aquariums are also very soothing and relaxing outings to take a child who is more sensitive to loud or bright events. Christian concerts too are great wholesome fun for the family.

Consider taking them to sporting events too. Zoe and Amelia love attending local minor league baseball games, and our local football team just opened a special room for kids on the autism spectrum at their stadium. In fact, one of our local play theaters also has a special room for little ones and kids with special needs. Look for these opportunities to allow your child to be engaged and explore cultural outings.

Education

The job of your child's high school is to prepare him or her for life as an adult. I have used my kids' IEPs to ensure they have a rich school life as well as opportunities for future employment. In my state, students with disabilities can attend high school through age 22. These "super seniors" are not in classes all that time but are on job sites and in various training programs as well.

You will want to sign up for all the programs they are eligible for as soon as possible. Your child's high school should be able to direct you to these programs. For example, in my state, there is an employment program for high-schoolers. I registered my daughter the day of her birthday so she could quickly get into the organization and participate in a work-study program.

Research local vocational schools that have a program for students with disabilities or autistic students, as well as colleges that run these programs. Some are full-fledged college programs while others are one-year programs designed to give your child a taste of the college experience. These are costly so you might want to start saving as early as you can.

You should also look at your state's offering for job programs for people with disabilities. We are blessed to live in a day and age where many education departments, companies, and organizations are creating employment opportunities for both people on the autism spectrum and those who are learning disabled. Our school district offers a work-based learning program designed to give children with special needs a taste of holding down a job during school hours. Look to see what local opportunities there are for you. For example, Bitty and Beau's is a coffeeshop chain that employs disabled people.

Your Child is an Integral Member of Society

One thing to remember is that your child is here for a purpose and that's not just to change your life. Your child has talents and gifts from God that can benefit others. Your child has the ability to work and share in the blessings of life. Don't deny him or her the opportunity. It will be difficult. You may be judged. You child may be judged.

Forget all that. Protect your child from those barbs, yes, but don't be ashamed or afraid to integrate him or her. Zoe and Amelia always have a good time when we take those chances, and they grow. Sitting home alone, like they did during the pandemic, stagnates them. It can even worsen any physical, mental, or emotional struggles they have. I've seen this firsthand. So take that step. Your child deserves to see all that this world has to offer, no matter what the naysayers say!

Chapter 17

Peace in the Trenches: Working through Transitions and Meltdowns

For this reason I bow my knees before the Father...that according to the riches of His glory He may grant you to be strengthened with power through His Spirit in your inner being. - Ephesians 3:14,16, ESV

The biggest challenge for your child is often going to be transitions: those times when getting from one place to another or changing from one activity to another leaves him or her disoriented and upset. Reactions range from meltdowns, to aggression, to self-injury or all three.

There are no easy answers or options for helping your child through this difficulty; however, it is critical that you remain calm enough to make wise choices. It's easy to get sucked into the maelstrom, and we've all been there. For years I found myself "crying on the kitchen floor" more often than I'd care to remember. You are only human, so rather than dwell on your mistakes of the past, forgive yourself and move ahead with more awareness and a plan in hand.

What can you do when these episodes happen? They can be dangerous for you, your child, and your family. Here are five steps you can take now to better manage your child's meltdowns and other difficult transition reactions.

Step 1: Calm Yourself First

Panic tends to spread quickly when your child has a meltdown. When Zoe experiences one, I am tempted to freak out or lose my temper. Additionally, at my daughter's height and weight (both bigger than me), I get nervous if she wants to hurt me because I've been injured in the past.

Unfortunately, elevated stress levels can escalate your child's stress, and that can start a vicious cycle that's hard to end. When your child loses her cool and comes after you, another family member, or even herself with biting, hitting, head-banging, or other aggressive and dangerous activities, you need to take steps to ensure that you remain as calm as possible.

The Art of Calming Down

Right off the bat, you may feel your blood pressure rise and your heart pumping harder. You may feel heated as stress levels soar and panic starts to set in. It's important to get a hold of your physical reactions immediately.

Step back and take a moment or two. First, slow your breathing to get your heart rate down. Then, set your mind on Jesus to get your body's stress reactions under control. Breathe in for eight seconds, hold for eight seconds, and slowly exhale for eight seconds. Focus on the name of Jesus as you do this.

Continue this for a few moments until your heart rate normalizes. As you do, ask the Holy Spirit to come into your heart and guide you. To maintain this calm, you may need something more. I advise you also pray aloud to keep your thoughts focused on the Lord while helping your child.

Praying aloud to the Lord is not just a good way to maintain your cool. It will also teach your child to cry out to the Lord in tough situations. Pray for wisdom, guidance, and the peace of Christ in this situation and hand it over to the Lord.

It can also be helpful to pray for the Lord to rebuke Satan and to help you resist him. Remember though, it's not necessarily Satan causing this issue, even if he is often behind your child's struggles. This may be a biological or psychological response to stress or other triggers. Keep praying, praising, and trusting Jesus with your words until you feel calmer and more stable.

Powering Through with God's Word

I have tried different approaches, and what has worked best during Zoe's meltdowns is to recite scripture. Memorizing scripture is tough for me, but years ago, I managed to memorize Colossians 3:1-17 (aka "Rules for Holy Living"). It took me almost a year and a lot of prayer for God's help to get it all down, but now, whenever I'm in distress, I can recite these "rules" and even put them into practice.

And if you are still hesitant, remember that there is power in God's word! 2 Timothy 3:16 says, "All scripture is God-breathed and is useful for teaching, rebuking, correcting and training in righteousness." I like that version best (NIV) because of that phrase, "God-breathed." Just as God breathed life into his creation, God breathes life into His very word. There is no tool that is more powerful to have in your life, especially as the mother of a child with severe autism, than placing the word of God in your heart, to take out and recite or pray when you are uncertain of how to help your child.

I believe that hearing the word of God can be a balm to your child, as well as to anyone within hearing range.

Short Scriptures You Can Memorize Today

If you don't have any scripture memorized yet, don't worry. First of all, if you know the Lord's Prayer (the "Our Father"), you *do* know scripture. This prayer is recorded in both Matthew 6:5-15 and Luke 11:1-3. Speaking these words aloud is one step you can take.

For other scriptures, take a few minutes daily to repeat short verses over and over. Recite one aloud eight times in a row over the course of a week or two, and you should have it memorized.

Here are several short verses that are easier to memorize:

- Colossians 3:2, NIV: Set your minds on things above, not on earthly things.
- Luke 6:31, NIV: Do to others as you would have them do to you. (*The Golden Rule!*)
- John 3:16, NKJV: For God so loved the world that He sent his only begotten Son, that whoever believes in Him shall not perish but have eternal life. (*This one is a little longer but if you've heard it many times before, that makes it more familiar.*)
- Philippians 4:4, NIV: Rejoice in the Lord always. I will say it again: Rejoice!
- Psalm 119:105, NIV: Your word is a lamp for my feet, a light on my path.
- Psalm 136:1, NIV: Give thanks to the LORD, for He is good. His love endures forever.
- Psalm 121:1-2, ESV: I lift up my eyes to the hills. From where does my help come? My help comes from the Lord, who made heaven and earth. (If you know the Casting Crown's song "Praise You In The Storm," this line is in the chorus. This song is very calming in times of crisis.)

If you regularly listen to Christian music, you probably know scripture verses from certain song lyrics. That's another option: start quoting Christian song lyrics that speak to you. Odds are good there will be a Bible verse in there.

Step 2: Make Sure Your Child — and Everyone Else — Is Safe

Meltdowns can pose a danger to your child. He may be banging his head on a wall or a table or biting his arm deep enough to break skin. It is possible that prayer and scripture can calm your child down, but that's not always the case. You need solid strategies to diffuse your child before anyone gets seriously hurt.

At this point, you should assess the situation. Think of yourself as your child's own personal first responder. Your job is to get your child to stop taking self-injurious actions without force because that can make things worse. This is why it's important that you are calm first. It's difficult to focus rationally on his or her safety if you are keyed up.

Be aware that you will be in harm's way. Your child may transfer their self-aggression to you or to someone else. Make sure that there is no one else nearby, unless it's another adult who has a trusted relationship with your child and is also aware of the risks, such as your spouse or a professional your child trusts.

There is no one good way to pull your child out of harming others or self-harm. You'll have to work with your child based on your own knowledge of past meltdowns. I can tell you from experience that if Zoe is biting her arm, trying to forcefully pull it out of her mouth will make things worse.

You also need to make sure to calm any nearby family members who have been triggered by your child's meltdown. You may need to tell other children to leave the room, put your baby in the crib, or put your dog outside, etc. Make sure that no one else is nearby if you're in public. The more you can contribute to creating a calm environment, the better.

Step 3: Protect Your Child

If you can, move to a safe area. For example, if your child is head banging, move him or her away from sharp edges. However, it's not always possible to get a child in a meltdown to move. If that's the case, then protect the area by doing things like throwing blankets or coats over dangerous surfaces. Enlist the aid of anyone nearby willing to help clear or protect your privacy. Right now it's important that your child has more space and less frustration.

Your mama instinct may be to hold and hug your child out of this. While it is important to engage your child affectionately in the way he or she finds acceptable, this is best reserved for when they are calm and back in control. Hugging too soon can make things worse, so stay back until you know you can approach your child safely.

Step 4: Find the Trigger to Fix or Avoid It

Every meltdown has a trigger, I believe, and the trick is finding it. Sometimes it's easy to discover or your child will tell you, either with words or by pointing. Other times, it's unclear.

This will be especially difficult if it's caused a physical issue you can't fix, such as a sound, smell, or light. Your best bet in that case is trying to relocate your child to avoid that trigger.

If you don't know what set your child off, review whatever has been a trigger in the past, such as harsh lighting like fluorescents, a particular song or scent, or an uncomfortable item of clothing. Think of everything that happened in the moments before the meltdown so that you can move to correct the situation.

For example, if he or she was triggered by a word or action from someone, have that person leave the area for a while, for example, a sibling may have taken away a toy.

I can't cover every cause and solution here. Just do your best to find the source of the problem so that you can address it and calm your child.

Step 5: Soothe and Distract

It's important to soothe and reassure your child with your words, even if he or she rejects you at first. Speak as gently and kindly as possible. Remember, this is not your child acting out but an uncontrollable physical response. Respect it as such.

With Zoe, it's particularly important that I say, "It's okay, you're okay," when she is upset. If you have a comforting phrase that you use with your child, you can repeat that over and over.

If possible, give your child something safe to bite or hit. In the moment of crisis, he or she may reject everything, even a favorite food. Some kids will not respond to this at all, so only make the offer if you think it might be an option. Be sure to pull back immediately if it makes things worse.

There are other ways to distract your child, like a favorite song or video, but remember, this is all about timing. If you introduce a distraction too soon, your child may become even more upset. In fact, that can actually make him dislike something he previously enjoyed and turn it into a trigger on its own.

That's why prayer is so important. Continue to pray for discernment and creative solutions for this crisis. The Holy Spirit can and will lead you safely out of this, but remember the enemy of your soul will tempt you with frustration, anger, and fear. Do not give Satan an inch, but let the Spirit guide you into peace in the middle of this storm.

Meltdowns and aggressive acts during times of transition are common, but with God's help and guidance, you can guide your child safely and securely out of this crisis.

Chapter 18

Nutrition and Your Child's Brain

He gives food to every living thing. His faithful love endures forever.
— Psalm 136:25, NLT

Most people have a complicated relationship with food, and our kids are no exception. All parents want the best nutrition for their families but as moms raising children on the autism spectrum, that can be a challenge. Our kids tend to be picky eaters, but that is only a small part of their dietary struggles. They also often have gut issues that impact everything from behavior to toileting, as well as food allergies or sensitivities. Some kids have celiac disease and others have food intolerances.

In fact, the impact of food on a child on the autism spectrum can be much more complicated than simply getting the basic recommended daily nutrition into our kids.

The old adage says, "You are what you eat." While that is true for everyone, it's even more crucial for the autistic brain – and gut. Science is revealing how food can and does contribute to autism and some of the challenges it presents.[1]

We learned this firsthand when we removed milk proteins, better known as caseins, from Zoe's diet. When she was five years old, she still had not achieved the coveted goal of sleeping through the night. That struggle weighed on us as a family, disrupting all of us.

We had tried all the conventional methods and recommended interventions: melatonin, nighttime routines, total darkness, nightlights, no distractions in the room, soothing color on the walls, etc. Nothing worked.

When a friend recommended removing milk products from her diet, I thought it was crazy, but I was desperate. An experienced doctor had told me two years earlier that the so-called "autism diet" was not worth the effort since there was no peer-reviewed proof that it worked at that time.

But when my friend said it would only take two to three weeks so I could try it temporarily, I knew it was worth a shot.

To this day, I do not think there has been a single intervention we've done that had so profound an impact on my entire family in so short a time. By her second week without cheese, cow milk, or other products with casein, Zoe was sleeping through the night! After that, I knew there was more to

1. https://scienceblog.com/508146/gut-bacteria-influence-autism-like-behaviors-in-mice

autism than what doctors at the time had been telling us and that everything my child eats is of critical importance.

The Autism Diet

The autism diet specifically is one where you eliminate some of the biggest problems for kids with gastrointestinal (GI) issues: caseins (cow milk proteins), gluten (the substance that gives bread its "gluey" nature), and soy (which can wreak havoc on hormones even if it USDA certified organic). Note that there are other restrictive diets, such as SCD, GAPS, Paleo, and Keto diets, which have been known to benefit kids with autism. The autism diet is a good starting point.

Additionally, you'll want to remove toxins, which means you may need to change out cookware, safe storage, BPA- and BPS-free containers, and no dyes, artificial flavor or preservatives, GMOs/bioengineered foods, or pesticides. Yes, it is a tall order, but it's worth the trouble. I'll go into more detail.

How the Autism Diet Can Benefit Kids on the Autism Spectrum

There are several reasons why the autism diet may help your child:

- Many kids with autism have allergies OR food sensitivities. Food allergies can be medically dangerous, cause anaphylactic shock and even be a cause of death in severe cases. The immune system is launching an attack against the food. Food sensitivities are as common but they don't get the same amount of press since they are often not deadly. These sensitivities arise when the body does not process food properly. This may happen if you are deficient in certain enzymes. While not life-threatening, sensitivities can cause problematic behaviors, medical issues, unprocessed nutrients, and other health issues.
- Good gut health is the key to a fully functioning immune system; however, many children with autism have gastrointestinal (GI) disorders. They often have problems with candida and other overgrowth of unhealthy flora or gut bacteria. Many of our children also have leaky gut and react poorly to glutens in their diet.
- Many kids on the spectrum cannot properly detox their bodies so when they are taking in foods or other products that have ingredients cause reactions, it doesn't process out of their bodies as easily as it does for the rest of us. These methylation issues can cause all kinds of problems for our children.
- Foods are linked to various issues. For example, artificial dyes can trigger ADHD behaviors in children. This could be part of the problem for your child. You need to look into his or her diet to pull out the offending foods and see the difference it makes.

Why the Autism Diet Might *Not* Work

You may have heard, "There's no clear evidence that the benefits outweigh the difficulties of such a diet" as our developmental pediatrician told us. What she really meant was at that time, there were no peer-reviewed studies that she could point to. Few, if any, had been done by 2000.

Today, there is a wealth of research demonstrating that a healthy gut is as important as a healthy brain and in fact, is crucial to brain development and maintenance. We now know about the importance of human microbiome and that poor gut health is linked to autoimmune issues. Additionally, gut and immunity are linked to healthy brain function.

Studies have been done on the impact of food and diets on autism and ADHD, a common challenge for people on the autism spectrum.

Still, you may hear people say, "The autism diet didn't work for me." It is actually exceedingly difficult to be 100 percent gluten free. If you pursue the diet but it doesn't seem to have an effect, there may be a reason for that:

Cross-contamination: This is probably the biggest reason why it's not working. In fact, "certified gluten free" is defined by the USDA to mean food items that can still contain 20 parts per million (PPM) of wheat, rye, barley, or crossbreeds of these grains unless otherwise noted.[2] Sounds little, right?

Well, for some kids, no gluten means literally zero PPM, not *even* 20 PPM. If a food had gluten removed or came into contact with a surface where gluten were processed, you may want to eliminate it. That means, for example, no oatmeal because it is grown with wheat. Certain milks are milled with gluten, and so you need to be on the lookout for glutens everywhere. Even at home, you cannot share surfaces like pots and pans where foods that are not gluten-free have been processed.

Your child hasn't been on it long enough: If it doesn't work after three months, your child may need to be off gluten for six months. If you still see no effect, but your child has autism and has had a benefit from being off casein, it's still likely that it somehow is benefiting him or her on a molecular or biochemical level you can't see. My advice is to just remain gluten-free. That can't hurt because you don't actually need gluten or grains, although the pasta lobby might beg to differ! (Yes, there is a pasta lobby, believe it or not.) What your child needs that pasta provides is fiber, and there is no better source than certain vegetables. Plus there are gluten-free pastas.

Unseen contamination: You have to really think outside the box with some products. It's possible your child's supplements have gluten. Or, perhaps you give your kid probiotics that contain some form of casein. Maybe you use hair care or bath products that contain gluten. I'm not just talking about skin absorption. My child has been known to drink bathwater! Or they may be getting it from a place you don't know — at school or daycare, from a friend, or they may be taking food at school when no one is looking. You'll need to ensure that these are not issues.

2. https://www.fda.gov/consumers/consumer-updates/gluten-free-means-what-it-says

Uninformed staff: Whether your child is at school, daycare, or other extracurricular activities, he needs to be monitored, and you have to make sure that the staff understands that even a little cheat is unhealthy. For kids in school, it's important to make this part of the IEP, but that is no guarantee that every provider is on board! One year, we discovered the speech therapist was giving my daughter dye- and sugar-laden sour candies as a reward. You must talk to each provider individually and make sure they know what to do and what not to do.

I also highly advise you to avoid food-based rewards in every venue and at home for your child.

Starting the Autism Diet

My recommendation is to move through this process one step at a time. First, remove caseins: that is, all products made with cow milk except organic ghee. (I'll go into detail about ingredients you need to avoid later in the chapter.) Do this for a few weeks (at least three) to see if any changes occur. Next, take out the gluten.

As mentioned, gluten is notorious for cross-contamination. The only way to remove gluten fully is to remove it 100 percent, down to the smallest microbe, and do that for three to six months. This is going to be a challenge and will take time and practice.

Soy which also should be removed, is challenging because it's in many processed foods, so the best way for success is to stop eating those as much as possible. If you cook with soy, you can substitute coconut aminos if you don't mind the taste. I find that adding salt and a bit of garlic and/or onion powder cuts down on the coconut flavor.

Anyone can do this on his or her own, but there are considerations. If your child has gastrointestinal (GI) issues such as diarrhea or constipation, they can affect his ability to properly metabolize nutrients including supplements. You should give your child the best nutrition you can, but without proper processing, he or she may not get the nutrients even with a healthy diet.

- *Costs:* This can be a costly diet if you strictly substitute gluten- and dairy-free packaged products for what you now eat. A better option is to cook fresh, wholesome foods more often. Processed food, even if it's organic and free from trigger foods, is still processed and loaded with preservatives and often sugar. In addition, it can be challenging for restaurants to get this right, so you may want to eliminate or cut down dining out or bring your kids' foods with you. What you save from those two things may make up for the extra costs of buying gluten-free flour and other items.
- *Benefits:* Restrictive diets allow you to discover what foods trigger behaviors, conditions like eczema, lack of sleep, diarrhea, constipation, and more. It's an effective way to find out what foods the rest of us can easily eat are harming your child even if he is not allergic to them. It can even be an easy fix that provides results

you had not imagined. For us, it helped us discover Amelia's dairy allergy and helped Zoe sleep through the night.

- *Downsides:* You need to be extremely diligent with your child's diet. As mentioned, we have stipulated in our daughter's IEP not to allow any food that doesn't come from home, but the rule has been broken from time to time. Second, you need to watch all the food your child has access to. You may need to do things like bring your own food to events your child is invited to. Sometimes people struggle and take insult with this. It's important to talk to friends and family about your child's food problems before you attend events. You just have to do what's best for your family and let the rest go.

  That said, as a Christian, you should always be gracious about these situations. Don't hog up your host's kitchen especially at a busy event. Try to bring food that is portable and easy to work with, and bring extra for anyone who wants to try your dishes. It's also true that some aspects of this diet can be a struggle. It's difficult to completely clear your child's gut of gluten, and it takes months. Even then you might not see an effect, but that doesn't mean changes aren't happening on a gut level. Patience and perseverance will reward you!

- *Risk assessment:* I don't really see any risks to this, but some people may freak out that you've stopped giving your child milk, including your pediatrician. Remember that your child needs calcium not "milk," and there are plenty of foods that you can get calcium from on a healthy diet. You may see a negative behavior or reaction or allergy disappear when that food disappears. That's why elimination diets are critical: You eliminate items, one at a time, for a recommended period of time and note the changes in your child.

- *Overall opinion:* I highly recommend this. The safest, fastest way to find out if a food is harming your child is to remove it from their diet—no false positives or negatives, no "scratch test" torture. Not all bodies are alike, and you cannot feed your child based on a chart provided by the government. Your child will not die or wither without dairy, gluten, or soy, and it just might help them thrive.

The Autism Diet in Depth

Let's take a deeper look at this diet. Often, you'll see the "autism diet" referred to as GF/CF or GF/CF/SF. Here are what those initials stand for and what that means in terms of diet:

GF: Gluten-Free: This diet is free of all wheat products and derivatives. There is controversy about the gluten content of certain grains (millet, sorghum, spelt), but anything that could be cross-contaminated should be eliminated. Hidden places you may find gluten include hot dogs, sausage, soy sauce, salad dressings, and more. It takes up to six months to clear the body of gluten.

CF: Casein-Free: Casein, the protein found in cow milk, is in all cow milk products. Ingredients to avoid include milk, cheese, casein/caseinate or any combination of that term, butter, butter fat, butter oil, many margarines, lacuose/lactulose, lactoglobulin, lactalbumin phosphate, pudding, nougat, goat's milk, any milk derivatives (condensed, solids, etc.), sodium lactylate, sour cream, sour cream solids, and whey in all forms. The following may contain casein: caramel, Bavarian cream, coconut cream, hot dogs, lunch meat, and sausages. Caseins take up to three weeks to remove from the body.

SF: Soy-Free (usually): Soy can mimic estrogen in the body, and it can be harmful, even when it's certified organic. It also can contain gluten, and it may wreak havoc on estrogen levels. Many artificial additives, emulsifiers, enhancers, etc. contain soy so beware. You are probably eating it even if you don't think so! For example, some olive oils are adulterated with soybean oil. Soy may clear the body in a few days.

The "Other" SF: Sugar: Some people use "SF" to mean sugar-free. The fact is your kids should be as sugar-free as possible! There's lots of controversy about natural sweeteners, but the basic rule is: Avoid white sugar (even organic), avoid products with "added sugar" or high levels of sugar, never use artificial sweeteners, and be judicious with fruits and more natural sweeteners such as maple syrup and coconut sugar. Not everyone can tolerate sweeteners such as xylitol, stevia, or monk fruit, which may upset the stomach.

This will be a struggle for many children, but sugar can lead to a host of gut problems, weight issues, addiction difficulties, health issues, and, of course, puts kids at risk for diabetes and cavities. Please reduce sugar as much as possible in your child's diet.

Foods to Avoid

Kids with autism (or really all kids) should also avoid the following foods for optimal brain health as much as possible:

- *GMOs or bioengineered foods:*[3] GMOs are banned in most of the European Union. Genetically modified organisms, or GMOs, are NOT like traditional hybrid foods. Hybrid foods are created when compatible plants are cross bred. GMOs are plants that are not compatible but the DNA has been forced together through a long and arduous process. For example, GMO corn has been cross bred with proteins that kill bugs, in order to protect the crop. Unlike hybrid plants, GMOs do not exist in nature. Scientists took a long time to "smash" the incompatible DNA into the corn and create this new breed, and then bred a new corn crop from it.
- To avoid GMOs, you either need to know which crops are not bred this way (yet) or eat certified organic or Non-GMO Verified crops.

3. https://nutritionstudies.org/gmo-dangers-facts-you-need-to-know/

Today, you can also look for the word "bioengineered" on the label, as this is how the U.S. Department of Agriculture (USDA) now designates these foods. However, I always assume that anything that is not certified organic or non-GMO verified likely contains GMOs.

- *Herbicide- and pesticide-treated foods:* Glyphosate is one of the most common crop herbicides, commonly sold in your hardware store as "Roundup." It is used on most if not all the wheat that is not USDA Organic certified in the USA. It can be on your produce too. It has been the source of contention for a long time, but in 2017, research from Europe showed it to be a possible carcinogen.[4] The courts have awarded millions to those who have claimed this chemical causes cancer. To avoid these, I recommend eating USDA Certified organic foods and produce as much as possible.

- *Artificial food coloring and dyes:* These have been linked to the symptoms of ADHD[5] and may even be implicated for more harmful health issues, like cancer[6]. If your child eats food with these, remove them to see if behaviors improve.

- *MSG:* This preservative is widely sprinkled on everything, especially in restaurants and in canned foods. Some people have physical reactions to it, like upset stomach or headache, but it's unclear if it causes more in-depth harm. The science on MSG is confusing. The FDA says it's safe, but they say that about a lot of foods and products they have not tested for harm. I think it's best to avoid MSG, since it's mostly found in unhealthy foods.

- *Artificial preservatives:* When we eliminated preservatives from Zoe's diet at age six, she moved from playing along alongside her peers (or "parallel play") to engaging with them. I've only met one other parent who experienced this phenomenon, but artificial preservatives are also harmful. They can cause allergic reactions and ADHD in children[7] and are linked to other health issues.

In short, fake food and toxic additives should be removed from their diet altogether. Whole foods and healthy eating is best!

Healing Diets for Children on the Autism Spectrum

What I've outlined for you is just a basic primer on using healthy diet to help your child through his or her behavioral, physical, and social challenges.

4. https://link.springer.com/article/10.1007/s00204-017-1962-5
5. https://pubmed.ncbi.nlm.nih.gov/17825405/
6. https://jamanetwork.com/journals/jamanetworkopen/fullarticle/2786028
7. https://www.scientificamerican.com/article/does-artificial-food-coloring-contribute-to-adhd-in-children/

There are several other more restrictive diets that have different functions for your child:

1. Ketogenic (Keto Diet) for autism. This is a specific protocol that you must do this diet with health practitioner, as it requires frequent testing and monitoring.
2. GAPS: Gut and Psychology Syndrome
3. SCD: Specific Carbohydrate Diet
4. AIP: Autoimmune Paleo
5. Low Oxalate
6. Low Phenols/Salicyate
7. Feingold Diet
8. Failsafe
9. Low FODMAPS
10. Body Ecology

For more information, I recommend the website NourishingHope.com, run by certified nutrition consultant and educator Julie Matthews, who specializes in nutrition and diets for both autism and ADHD. Julie is highly credentialed and has both a book and a course on the topic. I consider her one of the leading experts in the field.

Another excellent resource on autism is Autism.org. They are one of the leading resources for autism research. Look for webinars taught by Kelly Barnhill, MBA, CN, CCN, another expert on diet and nutrition who provided a wealth of knowledge and information for me when I started this journey.

Chapter 19

Detoxing Your Child

Or do you not know that your body is a temple of the Holy Spirit within you,
whom you have from God? You are not your own, for you were bought with a
price. So glorify God in your body. — 1 Corinthians 6: 19-20, ESV

Some years back, I was in a discussion with someone who firmly believed that autism is strictly genetic. I thought that was interesting because there is so much evidence today that makes a compelling case for the environmental causes contributing to the rise in numbers of kids diagnosed with autism. At the time, I began to wonder whether autism might be caused or triggered by environmental factors when specific genetic conditions are met.

Where is this evidence? Let's take a look at the latest research and the clues it provides. Please note that this is not an exhaustive overview, but it will give you an idea.

Back in 2015, researchers studied the genes of eighty-five families who had two children with ASD. While it is possible that genetic factors contribute, this study showed that even when siblings have autism, they do not share the same genetic risk factors. In other words, there are enough differences in siblings who have an autism diagnosis that something other than genetics may be coming into play. [1]

On the other hand, many twin studies show that autism has a high degree of heritability but recent studies show "a much higher contribution from non-genetic factors than was previously thought."[2]

According to Stephen M. Edelson, Ph.D., Executive Director, Autism Research Institute, an activated "autism gene" as a cause is only responsible for a small percentage of people on the autism spectrum. [3]

Today, many researchers agree that for the majority of cases, genetics plays a role but an environmental factor contributes as well. What is an "environmental factor"? It's anything that a fetus or baby is exposed to from his or her environment: food, chemicals, viruses, etc. If a child has a genetic predisposition for autism at this stage, toxic exposure can tip the scale towards autism.

[1.]   https://www.nature.com/articles/nm.3792
[2.]   https://www.autism.org/genetics-the-environment-and-autism
[3.]   Ibed

136

Why do these toxins affect some babies and not others? To understand that, we need to understand the basics of two scientific terms: epigenetics and methylation.

What is Epigenetics?

It's an ugly word, isn't it? It sounds scary—and complicated—but bear with me. This is really important for anyone raising a child on the autism spectrum!

Back in school, we all learned about DNA being the building blocks of life. DNA is a molecule that carries the genetic instructions (passed from mother and father) to develop a living organism, in this case, a human being. DNA is hard coded with these instructions.

However, those genes then get to "express" themselves. The DNA doesn't change, but the way the genes turn on and off can. The website WhatIsEpigenetics.com defines it this way: "Epigenetics is the study of mechanisms that switch genes on or off. It is involved in every aspect of life and such reversible, heritable changes affect the way we live as well as our future generations."[4]

The key takeaway here is that your genes are not static. Genetics and environmental exposures can turn genes on and off.

There may be other methods that flip these switches, but DNA methylation is the one that is most commonly referenced. Basically, methylation is the process that helps you detox things that should not be in your body.

Our bodies are smart. They know that when we ingest something that should not be in our systems, it has to get out. If not, it may accumulate and cause damage. For example, if aluminum, which is toxic for your brain, entered your body when you had water, medication, food, or vaccine that contained small amounts of it, a typically healthy person should be able to "pass" it. That's the job of the methylation system.

But if that system is not functioning properly, the heavy atoms of that metal can stay in your body and bind to places where they can accumulate and do harm, like your brain.

A Little More Science

Okay, just a little bit more so you can fully understand this process and how it might have impacted your child.

News Medical describes that DNA methylation is: "vital to healthy growth and development, it also enables the expression of retroviral genes to be suppressed, along with other potentially dangerous sequences of DNA that have entered and may damage the host."[5]

---

4. https://www.whatisepigenetics.com/fundamentals/
5. https://www.news-medical.net/life-sciences/What-is-DNA-Methylation.aspx

When the methylation process develops improperly, it can switch gene sequences on or off improperly so that it interrupts that methylation cycle. This has far-reaching consequences. According to the website DrJockers. com, "Methylation is involved in almost every bodily biochemical reaction and occurs billions of times *every second* in our cells."[6]

Poor methylation can contribute to the development of many chronic conditions, including the development of autism.

In other words, it's possible that your child was not born with autism but that it was triggered through a breakdown in the development of the methylation system at some point, pre- or postnatally.

The Benefit of Detox

One way to help restore proper function and prevent further bodily harm is to detox the system. Detox is the act of removing or blocking any and all harmful substances from the body.

Unfortunately, every single person in the developing world today is exposed to toxins on a frequent basis. Everyday things that are toxic for you include:

- Food that contains GMOs, pesticides, or additives, as discussed in the past chapter.
- Toxins in water or soil, including harmful chemicals in tap water, such as heavy metals, prescription drugs, and other elements.
- Bath, beauty, personal, and cleaning products that have untested chemicals in them or are "greenwashed." (That is, they claim they are safe but still contain harmful ingredients.)
- Toxins in the air from pollution and geo-engineering.
- EMF radiation, caused by Wi-Fi (More on this in the next chapter.)
- Stress and anxiety that harm your physical and mental health.

As you can see, our bodies are surrounded by an onslaught of unhealthy things that require a well-functioning methylation system. The inability to properly remove these toxins from your body is only one problem impacted by poor methylation. A healthy immune system can be damaged as well. To understand that, we need to learn more about a healthy gut.

The Role of Gut Bacteria

Inflammation is another significant issue and that be triggered by a malfunctioning methylation process and may contribute to the development of autism. If you notice that your child has a puffed-out belly or often suffers from eczema, these may cause inflammation caused by an imbalance in the gut bacteria. For example, your child's gut may be overrun with *candida*.

---

6. https://drjockers.com/understanding-methylation/

Immune system problems range from your child getting sick too often to never getting sick, like my own daughter. A healthy child will get sick one or two times a year to develop proper immunity. The good news is that a healthy immune system is attainable by using safe and natural ways to build immunity once it is functioning properly.

What does compromised gut bacteria look like besides a bloated tummy? Other symptoms can include:

- Difficulty eating or picky eater
- Constipation
- Runny stools or frequent diarrhea
- Difficulty potty training
- Sporatic laughter, almost like your child is drunk (I can remember a few times when Zoe was little that she'd be asleep but would start giggling uncontrollably.)

These problems cannot be solved with a daily dose of laxatives when an improper balance of gut bacteria causes them. In fact, according to *Scientific American*, studies have shown that the microbes found in the gut of kids with autism differ from those found in kids who did not have autism. [7]

The Science on Autism

When Zoe was little, autism was considered a developmental, lifelong disorder. But today, we know that children with severe autism commonly have these problems as well:

- GI tract issues
- Immune system problems
- Gut bacteria imbalances
- Problems with metabolism
- Problems with methylation

There is help for the difficult medical issues and complex behaviors that come with autism when you treat the body. Epigenetics gives us hope that we can "reprogram" these genes. Alternative therapies give us hope that we can detox our kids in the meantime. Natural approaches to health and real food intervention, like the autism diet or more restrictive type, can improve certain behaviors and relieve gut pain.

The paradigm is shifting, but it needs parents willing to take a chance and to do more. We need to stop telling parents there is no hope outside of ABA therapy. Many kids with autism have suffered gut pain for so long, they are not even aware of it. That pain manifests in behaviors like self-injurious behaviors or lashing out, especially when a child can't communicate.

[7.] https://scienceblog.com/508146/gut-bacteria-influence-autism-like-behaviors-in-mice/

However, it is difficult to discover and address the root issues. I've learned the hard way that it can take many specialists and many tactics. I advise finding a functional nutritionist or practitioner well-versed in autism if you want to consider detoxing your child.

And even then, you will still need to make your choices within your means, budget, abilities, and personality and of course, hand-in-hand with the Lord. It is a journey of many steps to find the path that most benefits each of our children so that he or she can have a life full of joy, family, friends, and a career, maybe even marriage.

And it is a journey that I will take with her every day of my life.

Chapter 20

Choosing and Using Technology with God's Wisdom

So we can confidently say, "The Lord is my helper; I will not fear; What can man do to me?" – Hebrews 13:6, ESV

Technology is all around us, growing faster and faster. It's often an especially useful tool for our kids as well. Text apps and learning devices, iPads, and GPS trackers aid our children and keep them safe. Apps can help them achieve all kinds of skills, including giving them a way to communicate.

But did you know there is danger lurking within many of these devices? It's not just in the tech that helps our kids. It's also in their schools, libraries, places of worship, activity centers, daycare providers, schools – and even in our homes and cars.

That danger is Electromagnetic Radiation – or EMF radiation, which all of us are exposed to daily. It's everywhere, and it's going to get worse.

What Is EMF Radiation?

First, let's talk about what EMF is. When you use any electronic devices, like computers or standard TVs, an electric current is generated that creates an extremely low frequency (ELF) electromagnetic field or EMF. Devices such as cell phones and tablets also transmit radio frequency signals (RF) when receiving data, text, and calls.

EMF radiation is a form of energy that can alter the environment, impacting your cells and can have negative health effects. Who is exposed to EMF radiation? Anyone who is using Wi-Fi, be it on a cell phone, tablet, smart TV, laptop or any other device that transmits and receives data. That means all our children are exposed to this radiation daily. But is it harmful?

The Dangers of EMF

The first time I ever heard about EMF was when I worked in telecommunications back in the 1990s. Our engineers told me something back then that many people are reluctant to hear today: exposure to EMF *can* cause serious health problems.

At night school, one of my computer science teachers told the class that he researched EMF for his doctorate and discovered that what comes out of the back of your television can cause illness. He had sage advice: "If you have children, never put their crib or bed the same wall as the television in the room next door."

At the time, the National Institute for Occupational Safety and Health published a fact sheet[1] revealing that people in certain fields who were exposed to elevated levels of EMFs in the workplace had higher rates of cancer.

Today, we have even more studies that reveal the harm of these fields of radiation. In 2016, U.S. National Toxicology completed a peer-reviewed study[2] proving that increased exposure to RF radiation led to a higher chance of rare brain and heart cancer. This is not the only study linking cancer and EMF exposure, but it is one of the largest and most in-depth and is well respected in the scientific community.

If you're wondering if our children are more vulnerable, the 2012 BioInitiative Report (see Bioinitiative.org) documented the effects of ELF and RF radiation on health. They concluded that these types of radiation have an adverse effect on fertility, reproduction, and children under the age of twelve.

Other studies have linked EMF to depression,[3] tumors,[4,5] childhood leukemia,[6,7] and breast cancer.[8] Pretty scary stuff for a mom to hear!

[1] " EMFs in the Workplace," DHHS (NIOSH) Publication Number 96-129, 1996, https://www.cdc.gov/niosh/docs/96-129/

[2] Report of Partial Findings from the National Toxicology Program Carcinogenesis Studies of Cell Phone Radiofrequency Radiation in Hsd: Sprague Dawley® SD rats (Whole Body Exposures), Michael Wyde, Mark Cesta, Chad Blystone, Susan Elmore, Paul Foster, Michelle Hooth, Grace Kissling, David Malarkey, Robert Sills, Matthew Stout, Walker, Kristine Witt, Mary Wolfe, John Bucher, https://doi.org/10.1101/055699

[3] Microwave frequency electromagnetic fields (EMFs) produce widespread neuropsychiatric effects including depression, Professor Emeritus of Biochemistry and Basic Medical Sciences, Washington State University, 638 NE 41st Avenue, Portland, OR 97232-3312, USA. https://www.ncbi.nlm.nih.gov/pubmed/26300312

[4] IARC Classifies Radiofrequency Electromagnetic Fields As Possibly Carcinogenic To Humans, World Health Organization, May 31, 2011, https://www.iarc.fr/wp-content/uploads/2018/07/pr208_E.pdf

[5] Evaluation of Mobile Phone and Cordless Phone Use and Glioma Risk Using the Bradford Hill Viewpoints from 1965 on Association or Causation, Michael Carlberg and Lennart Hardell, Biomed Res Int. 2017; 2017: 9218486.

[6] A pooled analysis of magnetic fields and childhood leukaemia. Ahlbom A1, Day N, Feychting M, Roman E, Skinner J, Dockerty J, Linet M, McBride M, Michaelis J, Olsen JH, Tynes T, Verkasalo PK. Br J Cancer. 2000 Sep;83(5):692-8.

[7] Electrical wiring configurations and childhood cancer. Wertheimer N, Leeper E. Am J Epidemiol. 1979 Mar;109(3):273-84.

[8] Residential and occupational exposures to 50-Hz magnetic fields and breast cancer in women: a population-based study. Kliukiene J1, Tynes T, Andersen A. The Cancer Registry of Norway, Institute of Population-based Cancer Research, Oslo, Norway.

To date there are over 1,000 studies on the impact of exposure to EMF. These studies were compiled by Joel M. Moskowitz, Ph.D, Director of the Center for Family and Community Health, School of Public Health, University of California, Berkeley. His overview of the studies at Saferemr. com suggest that a full 89 percent of these studies have significant impact on oxidative stress, a cellular process which harms the body's ability to detox the harmful effects caused by free radicals. 73 percent of the studies report significant neurological effects and 54 percent of the studies show an impact on DNA.

EMF and Autism

As mentioned, our kids benefit from their devices. For example, those who struggle with communication now have a voice, thanks to these devices. But are they being harmed by their EMF exposure?

Dr. Martha Herbert, whose work is well known to some parents in the autism community, has published a peer-reviewed study called, "Autism and EMF? Plausibility of a pathophysiological link, Part I[9] and Part II.[10]" She states that kids with autism are subject to "major weak points" and one of those is EMF. She believes that some of the behaviors apparent in autism can be aggravated by EMF exposure. That is, children on the autism spectrum may be even more susceptible to the dangers of EMF radiation than children who are not.

Eight Ways to Reduce the Dangers of EMF

If you're now thinking you'd like to toss your phone out the window, stop! The fact is that even if you do, you are still going to be subject to EMF radiation from your neighbors and others around you. As we keep upgrading our grids both nationally and globally, we need to take precautions to protect our children.

Protection From EMF

Fortunately, there are a few simple measures that you can take to keep your family safe and that includes keeping your devices at a distance. EMF exposure accumulates. That means that the longer you are exposed and the closer you are to your devices, the more likely you will suffer health consequences.

These are some steps you can take to reduce your family's exposure to EMF:

1. Keep your Wi-Fi router set up as far away as possible from your family living and sleeping areas as possible – like in the garage or basement.

---

[9] https://wwwncbi.nlm.nih.gov/pubmed/24095003
[10] https://wwwncbi.nlm.nih.gov/pubmed/24113318

2. Turn off the Wi-Fi at night, every night. Set it up so that it's easy to accomplish, keeping everything organized and in one place. You can buy a low-budget timer and schedule it to turn off at night and on in the morning.

3. Keep all cell phones and tablets devices away from your bedroom at night.

4. When possible, hardwire your TV, computers, and other large electronics rather than using Wi-Fi. Play as many things as you can through a hardwired TV. That will allow your family to stay safer during work or play.

5. Don't add more large-scale electronic devices that can't be hardwired or turned off to your home. (Do you *really* need a Wi-Fi-connected refrigerator?) You may also want to reconsider using any baby monitors as they may be harmful.

6. Limit how much time your child spends on cell phones and tablets. You know you want to reduce their screen time– now you have an excellent health reason! Don't forget that they are also spending time on devices at school.

7. Don't get too close. Try not to carry your cell phone on your person too often, using a purse or bag. Use a hands-free headset or put it on the table in a docking station to create some distance when using. At just one foot away from the source, the EMF emissions decrease in strength. And those emissions leaving the mobile device and heading away from you are not as harmful as the ones in direct contact with your body.

8. If you use mobile electronic devices directly against your body, EMF radiation shields should be used to help limit your exposure. Do not put your laptop on your lap without a shield! What I mentioned above about the back of a TV holds true for the back of other devices too.

9. When using technology, you should also use a blue light filter at night. Blue light from phones and tablets can disrupt sleep patterns and have other consequences for kids on the spectrum. You can set this up on your phone or computer (if they are not old) and schedule it to automatically turn on when the sun sets.

10. If you have a smart meter from your electric company, you can buy a shield to protect yourself. If possible, do not upgrade to a smart meter. (Be aware that some companies are automatically installing these without your consent even when state or local laws require consumer consent.)

There are also many ways to counter the harm from EMF. Earlier I mentioned that EMFs cause oxidative stress. You may want to find a protocol that reduces this kind of stress on your child. Hyperbaric oxygen therapy and infrared saunas are two examples. Do your research or speak to a functional practioner to learn more.

Managing Technology

As I said, our kids benefit from technology so I do not recommend eliminating all devices from their lives. With the modern education system and workforce, this isn't possible anyway. If they don't know how to work a phone or a tablet, they won't be able to work or socialize.

The best course of action is to set rules for your child about how long he or she can be on their phone or tablet per week and what you will and will not allow. And don't forget to include school computer time! Like any other child, setting a solid foundation now will help your child continue a balanced screen time routine as he grows to adulthood.

On many devices, you can set limits on time spent or what they can see, however, do not just rely on the device to manage their media exposure. Some videos have age-safe ratings but still allow things that are inappropriate for a child including profanity. You don't want to hover over your child all the time but you should pop in once in a while to see what they are viewing. You may need to eliminate some shows or music choices.

My personal preference is to keep my kids off social media altogether. Between cyberbullying, identity theft, and pedophiles, unsupervised online interaction through social media can be dangerous even with the supervision of a savvy, cautious parent. Be wise and ask for the Lord to lead you to discern what you should and should not allow for your child.

I kept Amelia and Zoe from getting their own phones for a long time. But inevitably, they then gravitated towards my phone or Chris' phone. Their school computers took dominance as well. Without phones, it's hard to build relationships in this day and age. So it's not realistic to keep your children off technology forever, but you should carefully manage what they are exposed to and for how long.

A Few Words about Fear

While these efforts are helpful, you might be afraid that EMF radiation is all around us, and you'd be right. There are toxins around us that we cannot avoid. Such are the consequences of living in a fallen world.

But while we cannot protect our children from every single toxic exposure, God does not want us to worry. The Lord knows what He's doing with us, with our child, and with this world. 2 Samuel 22:31-32 (ESV) says:

> *This God – His way is perfect; the word of the Lord proves true. He is a shield for all those who take refuge in Him. For who is God, but the Lord? And who is a rock, except our God?*

It's not *just* that there is nothing He cannot handle. We may live in a fallen world with dangers and snares all around us but Jesus is walking with us, hand in hand. We are not bequeathed a legacy of fear, but of strength – *His* strength, in His name alone, if we trust Him completely.

And here are few reminders that will hopefully calm your fears about exposure to EMFs and other toxins or dangers your child may encounter when you are trusting in the Lord's protection.

- God has appointed the date when we will die. Psalm 139:16 says, "Your eyes saw my unformed substance; in your book were written, every one of them, the days that were formed for me, when as yet there was none of them." Taking care of your health does not change the date of your death but it can impact the quality of your life and your child's life.
- For those of us who have eternal life, while the thought of dying may be scary, what immediately follows is peace, joy, and everlasting love as we run into the arms of our Savior. Don't worry as much about saving your child's earthy life as improving their health. Instead, think about how to use your time to help your children — and others — find life eternal.
- As Hebrews 13:6 says, "So we can say with confidence, 'The Lord is my helper, so I will have no fear. What can mere people do to me?'" The Creator of the universe is your Helper, your Father, and your Friend. You have nothing to fear because everything that comes into your life is overseen by Him and brought forth for your good (Romans 8:28) and His glory (Isaiah 42:8). Even if God allows your child to get sick, there is a purpose in that, just as He has a purpose in allowing your child to be on the autism spectrum. He allows different circumstances for His glory, your spiritual maturation, and your testimony.

As we walk forward in a world corrupted by evil on every level — physical, chemical, spiritual, cultural, etc. — we can trust that we have nothing to fear as long as we stay close to our Savior. However, we must do our best to make the choices that are appropriate for the health of our families.

Chapter 21

Finding Hope When Nothing Seems to Be Improving

Therefore, my beloved brothers, be steadfast, immovable, always abounding in the work of the Lord, knowing that in the Lord your labor is not in vain.
— 1 Corinthians 15:58, ESV

Are you at the end of your rope? Do you feel like you have tried everything and nothing is getting better for your child?

Boy, do I know how that feels! In fact, I'm in the midst of this right now. What do you do when the Lord doesn't seem to want to heal your child? It's challenging and painful but there is a way through. In fact, I would say that the Lord does want to heal your child, but perhaps not in the time or the way that you would.

As I've said, I believe that many of the negative medical, social and behavioral issues are environmental. It's important to keep in mind that when you're dealing with autism, you're also dealing with a moving target. Things that were solved yesterday may again be a problem today, and things that were never an issue may suddenly crop up. Environmental factors change and come into play over and over as your child is exposed or his or her body chemistry changes, with or without your knowledge. This includes things like puberty, diet, nutrition, your child's biochemistry, gut bacteria, ability to naturally detox, reaction to a supplement or medication, etc.

You're going to find people who have gotten every single issue under control for their child, while some of those things you may never solve. That's what it seems like to me with a few of Zoe's more concerning challenges. We have tried everything: homeopathy, supplements, medicine, behavior modification, prayer, you name it, nothing seemed to work.

In these times, your faith may be flagging. And that is the real problem. Who will get the glory if and when you heal your child?

What to Do When Nothing Is Working

Okay, so now what? Troubling issues bring plenty of stress to parents like us. Some of these issues can have profound consequences. As an autism parent, you may have envisioned horrible scenarios for today and the future. I know I have. What are you going to do next?

Before we go further, your first plan of action should be to make sure you haven't missed anything. Here are some actionable steps you can take while you seek guidance for caring for your child:

Leave No Stone Unturned

First, make absolutely certain you have left no stone unturned. As I said before, the level you can intervene at will depend on your budget. I'm not suggesting you go into debt to treat your child. That can have ramifications of its own, and you might be better off leaving that money for his or her future.

Often, though, you might not have done something that you didn't realize. Or, your child has reached a level of independence you didn't imagine and is now doing something new – like swapping food with other children. Another issue is that protocols may be interfering with each other, or some kind of condition is blocking everything from working. For example, if your child cannot extract nutrients properly, it will do her no good to take typical vitamins.

Be sure to thoroughly investigate all those options. You might want to do an in-depth testing panel or work with a functional practitioner, doctor, or other expert, especially one that specializes in autism.

Find the Vocabulary

In order to make sure you've not left anything out, you have to know the terminology of what you are talking about. This is the time to hit up autism sites and resources, as much as possible. I recommend TACANOW.org and Autism,org, which has information laid out in easy-to-read sections that any parent can use.

I also recommend you ask other moms whom you trust about the issues that you can't seem to solve. They might have insight into why a certain treatment was not working for them and how they resolved it. And do your best to find the vocabulary that is used for this or that condition. Words are powerful, and they help you to be accurate when talking with your doctor or practitioner as well as when you are researching information and treatments.

Reach Out to Your Tribe

Hopefully you've found some support by now, but if not, reach out for help from the resources I listed in Chapter 8. You will need that support, especially now. Even when autistic children look and seem extremely different, even when they are years apart, the journey may have similar components that are familiar to all of us. (Zoe collects rocks, maybe your child likes sticks, but either way, they are loading up their schoolbags with junk they don't need!) One such conversation let me know that I was not alone in a struggle we were facing and that it was a toileting condition that had a name. Yes, those other parents can even help you get a proper diagnosis for your child's challenges.

Be Gentle with Your Child

As a particular toileting problem escalated and worsened for my child, my anxiety went through the roof. Part of that stress was because I couldn't find the solution, and part was because I was frustrated with having to take care of this issue repeatedly.

My frustration at the situation turned into frustration at my daughter – for an issue she cannot help. As parents, we need to learn to gather our wits whenever dealing with unsolvable issues that cause us so much tension. Slowing down and remembering this is not her fault helped me to stop yelling and treat my daughter with more kindness and respect.

Accept Things as They Are

Of course, calming down only really pushed the problem elsewhere. I took that pent up stress out on my husband – not the best solution. That's because I had not accepted that this was something incurable.

Really, deep down, I still believe the problem can be solved, but for whatever reason, God is not letting me see that answer. Maybe it'll just clear up one day but at present, I have to equip my daughter to handle this toileting issue in a way she can manage herself. Her independence and self-reliance are the most important things here.

Examine Yourself

Since I first wrote this, God has confronted me with His will - and my impatience. I will make this long story short by saying that in my heart, I knew - and still know - what God has wanted me to do to help my child.

However, I have resisted. Or I should say, I have disobeyed Him.

My child's issues will never be resolved on a simplistic gluten-free diet. She needs much more intensive care for her microbiome, the kind I feel ill-equipped to manage. I actually cannot stand cooking. It's one of my least favorite tasks. Add to that my difficulty remembering concepts and the complexity of nutrition for autism and her delicate system, and you see that I have a problem.

This is humiliating for me to admit, but honestly, what I "thought" was my best for my child simply wasn't. It's not that I wasn't trying multiple interventions, doing my research, praying and trusting the Lord. I was. And I was working hard on other things too: self-care, housework, kids' programs, their schooling, reading Scripture to them, praying for and over them, my marriage, church attendance, volunteering, etc.

But deep down, I was avoiding the one thing I knew in my gut would help her - a more restrictive diet - because I thought it would be too hard. And I was avoiding other things too: spending real quality time with them, teaching them housekeeping, and teaching the more difficult aspects of hygiene.

I failed them.

And to be brutally honest? I was using protocols as a way to shortcut the more difficult tasks. But God didn't give up on getting through to me. We'd been through a long and extended period of difficulty and had come through it. When things got better, that's when the darkness hit me.

I was unable to sleep because of it. It was as heavy as a weight on my chest, and to be honest, it freaked me out. I did all kinds of things before getting out of bed, pulling out my Bible, and getting on my knees.

And there, God confronted me with my own disobedience.

Because I was still lying to myself in order to avoid more challenges, I was stunned. Wasn't I already doing everything? Of course, I knew that was not true. I was in slipshod on lots of things. The prior few months had been so incredibly stressful that I could not do a proper diet - or any of the things I'd promised for taking care of for my children. And God convicted me that this was a result of my disobedience.

You see, I'd needed this correction all along but I was dealing with too much stress from broken situations for God to confront me until they were past. God knows we can only handle one correction at a time and, in times of extreme stress or heartache, not even that.

And in all honesty, our family went through a several-month crisis that needed to be resolved before I could put both feet into a healing diet. I am still struggling. I'm even tempted to say a clean diet is impossible but with Him, we know that nothing is impossible.

Not my frozen response. Not my laziness. Not my comfort, or my sins that really look like "no big deal" but keep me from being the mother God calls me to be.

And in the end, the Lord taught me if and when there is healing to be done, He will do it. Now, of course, we need to do our part, just like we can't sit on the couch, eat what we want, and pray to God to get us in shape.

In the same way, the Lord has blessed us with some tiny forward motion in my daughter but He's leaving the heavy lifting to me. I do the work, then He will do the healing.

While we know our labor is not in vain, ask yourself: have I done everything I know to do or am I hiding something that I'm not willing to take on? Has the Lord challenged you to go the distance for your child? Is there something you're not telling yourself because you don't want to face what it would mean for your priorities?

If you're not sure, ask the Lord to reveal what you are getting wrong. And if you are hiding an unpleasant truth in your heart, get it out there. Confess and be free, then do the work that is more challenging so God can bless you and your family.

Keep Hope Alive

Finally, and this is critical for your heart: Never give up hope! The Lord has placed this issue in your life for a reason.

Yes, this is difficult but we are getting through it. Zoe is a blessing to us, and I am thankful every day for her. She has a purpose, and I am fully committed to helping her have the fullest life she can have. There is really no limit to other things that she can do – and that's true for all children, whether or not they have disabilities.

We are all weak in areas. Some, like me, in many areas. Satan will call you a bad mother, the wrong mother, he'll tell you that this or that can't be done.

But we all have strengths, gifts, and talents that we can use to be a blessing to those around us, and our children are no different. Don't let the difficult challenges of raising an autistic child get in the way of helping your child live to the best of their abilities, and never give up hope that they can't grow into a productive, loving member of society. It's all possible with God's help.

Chapter 22

God's Purpose for Your Challenges

To console those who mourn in Zion,
To give them beauty for ashes,
The oil of joy for mourning,
The garment of praise for the spirit of heaviness;
That they may be called trees of righteousness,
The planting of the Lord, that He may be glorified.
— Isaiah 61:3, ESV

When my beautiful Zoe was born, I was not yet a Christian. And then things became so difficult at home that church became an escape for me. But the Lord had bigger and better plans, and weekly exposure to God's word and solid preaching led me to the I had completely rejected.

And eventually, that led to reliance on Jesus to get through my challenges.

The problem was I was still leaning on myself. And when the truly tough stuff showed up, I turned away, drowning it out one way or another, with selfish desires: food, drink, games, books, the gym, anything to hide from reality.

Sometimes, I did turn to God, reading my Bible or listening to sermons. One time, I actually took extensive notes on Nehemiah with the thought to create a bible study for moms raising a child on the spectrum. Imagine my shock and horror when I lost that notebook.

I couldn't understand why.

And then, the worst thing ever happened to me.

I cannot share the details at this time, but let's just say this was a problem that I had turned a blind eye to for a long time because I was too selfish to do what needed to be done to face the problem. My world fell apart. I thought I'd hit bottom and I still couldn't face it. Turned out, it wasn't the bottom yet. A few months later, Covid-19 lockdowns took that already enflamed situation and blew it up.

I came to the lowest point in my life and my family suffered a great deal, especially my daughters.

For the next year and a half, I tried extremely hard to follow God. As usual, I tried to do the right thing, following advice given to me by Godly friends and family. But nothing seemed to help.

I tried a million and one spiritual things too. Doing my own personal Bible studies, meeting anyone and everyone I could on Zoom, stepping out of my comfort to share my faith, and speaking truth to people.

And then, a friend and I attended a presentation by a chiropractor on the fight or flight response. I almost fell out of my chair when he described the symptoms of post-traumatic stress disorder (PTSD) because it explained things I'd been dealing with for more than three years that I could not understand.

Wait, what?? Me? PTSD?? But I was happy, wasn't I? I was doing all the things I was supposed to, right? Self-care, prayer, family, Bible reading, church, sermons, all the things, yes?

But there was one thing I had not done: surrendering it all to God.

I know: Surrender is something we talk about a lot. We sit in church and sing, "I Surrender All," thinking we mean it. Or, maybe we think how old-fashioned that song is.

We accept what the bible says outwardly but the niggling doubt in our heart "*God couldn't want me to be this miserable, could He?*" is a sign that we don't trust Him fully.

Because the truth is, most of the time *we don't.*

We may have a bumper sticker that reads, "Let go and let God," but do we?

On the surface, it looked like I had done the right things but deep down, I was still clinging to trust in my own ability to make a change that only Jesus could make. And that's why I was suffering so much stress. I was begging the Lord night after night to fix a situation without truly trusting that He could.

When I came home from that event, everything changed. First, I admitted that I had PTSD. For years, I had shared numerous studies that show parents raising kids with special needs are prone to PTSD, but had not seen it for myself until I recognized the symptoms.

The crisis in my life demanded I make some decisions, and plenty of people advised me on what to do. But recognizing PTSD finally made me take action: I turned to God by taking to my knees and begging Him to give me direction, loud and clear – and with confirmation.

Within a night, I had my answer. I was doing my nightly Bible reading, when I read a footnote about the apostle Paul. This led me to read the last letter that Paul wrote, 2 Timothy. When I read the meat of that letter, I came away with a simple message from God: we are not here for our own comfort or pleasure but do what God wills us and leave the rest to Him.

Paul himself is one of the best examples of this. He was chased, beaten, arrested, imprisoned, flogged, shipwrecked, his name besmirched, he was local gossip, he'd been betrayed and abandoned by friends, and finally, sentenced to death.

But he didn't complain about any of that. What did he say about the hardships of his life? In Philippians 1:21-26, he reveals this truth:

For to me to live is Christ, and to die is gain. If I am to live in the flesh, that means fruitful labor for me. Yet which I shall choose I cannot tell. I am hard pressed between the two. My desire is to depart and be with Christ, for that is far better. But to remain in the flesh is more necessary on your account. Convinced of this, I know that I will remain and continue with you all, for your progress and joy in the faith, so that in me you may have ample cause to glory in Christ Jesus, because of my coming to you again.

There we have it. Paul was happy to die, to be with Christ, but joyful to live a difficult and uncomfortable life to bring more people to Christ. We will never know how many souls Paul brought to the Lord, in life, in death, or with the Holy-Spirit inspired words he left behind, but we do know he did not waste time wallowing in his pain. He always moved forward, calmly, on the path Jesus laid out for him.

God made it clear to me that I'm exactly where I need to be, even if some well-meaning Christian friends disagree. Walking this path was painful, and it came with some real challenges, like PTSD. But what can the Lord bring from it?

You see, God is not just working in your life on your behalf. He's creating a story out of your experiences to share with others who are in crisis too.

So I accepted the path He put me on, casting aside all thought as to whether or not I "liked" it. I realized, though, very quickly, that this path was full of problems that were out of my hands. I wasn't supposed to try and fix things. My purpose was to pray, support, and shine the light of Jesus.

That is where I learned to put all my trust in the Lord.

I know you are hurting. I know you are desperate. I know the world feels like it lies in shattered pieces around your feet and there's nothing more you can do. You need to surrender it.

The question is, how? In these next two chapters, I'm going to share two stories in the Bible that helped me with the next leg of my journey.

Chapter 23

Abraham and Isaac: A Story of Surrender

Whoever loves father or mother more than Me is not worthy of Me, and whoever loves son or daughter more than Me is not worthy of Me. – Matthew 10:37, ESV

We are often told to "let go and let God," to surrender our burdens. What actions can we take to do that?

Now we're going to take a look at one of the most disagreeable stories in the bible. In Genesis 22, the Lord asks Abraham to sacrifice his only son. If you're unfamiliar with it, you'll quickly understand why it's such a contentious and difficult scripture.

The story of Abraham in Genesis is amazing. It lays out how God made a covenant with this one man to set up the Israelite nation and religion. His story starts in Genesis 12. Despite being the son of a pagan, the Lord appeared to a man named Abram and made promises to grow his lineage into a great nation. He decided to follow the Lord and did what He asked without debate. In chapter 17, God makes a formal covenant with him, and changes his name to Abraham; in chapter 18, he promises him a son despite the fact both he and his wife are long past child-bearing age.

God is faithful to His promise, and in chapter 21 Isaac is born to a post-menopausal Sarah, whose body is so completely restored that she can breastfeed the baby. Experts mostly agree that biblical clues place Isaac's age at the time of the story we'll study was that of a young man.[1] It's not important to know Isaac's exact age as to understand he's not a little boy in Genesis 22.

Let's think about Isaac too. Imagine if you wanted a child and every doctor you had ever seen told you it was impossible. Then, you went through menopause, so you knew you'd never have a child, but then you did get pregnant. That's how Sarah and Abraham learned that with God, nothing is impossible.

Having a child by supernatural means must have been something that the whole family – the whole *town* – talked about. Surely Abraham shared the story with his son. I bet Sarah doted on Isaac, telling how special he was to the Lord. While the Bible does not specifically state this, I think any parent in this situation would share with their child the Lord's promises for him.

[1.] https://www.gotquestions.org/how-old-was-Isaac.html

Keep this in mind as we look at the events of Genesis 22:1 to 19, NKJV. Let's start with the first two verses. (Feel free to read the full text first if you like.)

> Now it came to pass after these things that God tested Abraham, and said to him, "Abraham!"
> And he said, "Here I am."
> Then He said, "Take now your son, your only son Isaac, whom you love, and go to the land of Moriah, and offer him there as a burnt offering on one of the mountains of which I shall tell you."

Right here, we have the Lord testing Abraham by telling him to sacrifice Isaac. God specifically says, "your only son Isaac, whom you love." This part of the verse calls to mind two New Testament scriptures. The first is John 3:16:

> For God so loved the world that He gave His one and only Son, that whoever believes in Him shall not perish but have eternal life.

God refers to Isaac as Abraham's only son, even though Abraham had an illegitimate son, Ishmael. In fact, before Isaac was conceived, Abraham had asked God why not use Ishmael to bring the great nation but is flatly turned down.

That's because God honors true marriage. Isaac, as the forerunner of the twelve tribes of the nation of Israel, had to be a legitimate, legal heir from Sarah. Ishmael was a son he had with a woman who was not his wife.

The next verse this brings to mind is Matthew 3:16-17, which describes Jesus' baptism.

> When He had been baptized, Jesus came up immediately from the water; and behold, the heavens were opened to Him, and He saw the Spirit of God descending like a dove and alighting upon Him. And suddenly a voice came from heaven, saying, "This is My beloved Son, in whom I am well pleased."

The Lord loves His Son, and is pleased with the action He is taking, and this brings to mind Abraham's love for his only son as well.

What is Abraham's reaction to the Lord's request? Genesis 22:3 says:

> So Abraham rose early in the morning and saddled his donkey, and took two of his young men with him, and Isaac his son; and he split the wood for the burnt offering, and arose and went to the place of which God had told him.

I want to pause at this verse for a moment because the contrast between these two sentences is important. In verse 3, Abraham is quick to obey the Lord and make preparations. One sentence details several actions, rising, prepping the donkey, bringing some help, chopping wood, etc. Six actions, one long verse. And yet, the next verse slows the cadence of action down completely.

> Then on the third day Abraham lifted his eyes and saw the place afar off. —Genesis 22:4

Verse 3 sounds like Abraham is doing all the busy work to keep his mind off of the Lord's assignment of sacrificing his son. But as he sees the site of the sacrifice in verse 4, Abraham pauses. Did he have a moment of hesitation? Was he thinking, "Am I really going to do this to my only son?"

He knew God kept His promises. He witnessed God bring the impossible to pass when Isaac was born. And he knew that God could be trusted to resolve this situation so that Isaac would remain his heir and the start of a great nation, as promised.

Abraham then kept moving. He knew that God would remain faithful to His promises. It took complete surrender to the Lord, but he would continue on the Lord's mission.

Why did Abraham do this? The answer is in Hebrews 11:17-19:

> By faith Abraham, when God tested him, offered Isaac as a sacrifice. He who had embraced the promises was about to sacrifice his one and only son, even though God had said to him, "It is through Isaac that your offspring will be reckoned." Abraham reasoned that God could even raise the dead, and so in a manner of speaking he did receive Isaac back from death.

Abraham had faith. He had seen what the Lord could do and would do, and he trusted Him completely. And so, he knew that the Lord would make this right, somehow, God would either save Isaac or bring him back from the dead to fulfill His promise.

One other thing is going on here. The site of the sacrifice is the location of the most important event in the Bible, better known to us as Calvary, where Jesus was crucified. It's no coincidence that the Lord had Abraham arrive on the third day. God provides for Abraham's sacrifice with a substitution, just as God provided Jesus as a substitute sacrifice for all humanity in order to clearly show in the Old Testament an illustration of what will happen in the New Testament.

Let's continue with Genesis 22:5-9:

> And Abraham said to his young men, "Stay here with the donkey; the lad and I will go yonder and worship, and we will come back to you."
> So Abraham took the wood of the burnt offering and laid it on Isaac his son; and he took the fire in his hand, and a knife, and the two of them went together. But Isaac spoke to Abraham his father and said, "My father!"
> And he said, "Here I am, my son."
> Then he said, "Look, the fire and the wood, but where is the lamb for a burnt offering?"
> And Abraham said, "My son, God will provide for Himself the lamb for a burnt offering." So the two of them went together.

> Then they came to the place of which God had told him. And
> Abraham built an altar there and placed the wood in order; and he
> bound Isaac his son and laid him on the altar, upon the wood.

Remember, most scholars believe that Isaac was a man at the time of this
event. Even if not, he was strong enough to carry all the wood and potentially
strong enough to overcome his father. Isaac hesitates, wondering where the
lamb is. His father — a bit cryptically — tells him the Lord will provide it. But
when they come to the spot, there's no mention of Isaac resisting or fighting
his father. We don't know what was said between them but this implies is
that Isaac willingly let himself be bound to that altar, reminding us again of
Jesus' willing sacrifice on the Cross.

God had made them a promise and both father and son knew that Isaac
would be the head of a great nation, through his heirs. They trusted that the
Lord would not strike Isaac down. So what happens next? Genesis 22:10-12:

> And Abraham stretched out his hand and took the knife to slay his
> son. But the Angel of the Lord called to him from heaven and said,
> "Abraham, Abraham!"
> So he said, "Here I am."
> And He said, "Do not lay your hand on the lad, or do anything to
> him; for now I know that you fear God, since you have not withheld
> your son, your only son, from Me."

Abraham did not withhold his only son, just as the Lord God did not
withhold His only Son, Jesus, to be laid out as a sacrifice. Of course, that
offering was completed, that we might have salvation. Let's finish this story
with Genesis 22: 13-19:

> Then Abraham lifted his eyes and looked, and there behind him
> was a ram caught in a thicket by its horns. So Abraham went and
> took the ram, and offered it up for a burnt offering instead of his
> son. And Abraham called the name of the place, The-Lord-Will-
> Provide; as it is said to this day, "In the Mount of the Lord it shall
> be provided."
> Then the Angel of the Lord called to Abraham a second time out of
> heaven, and said: "By Myself I have sworn, says the Lord, because
> you have done this thing, and have not withheld your son, your
> only son — blessing I will bless you, and multiplying I will multiply
> your descendants as the stars of the heaven and as the sand
> which is on the seashore; and your descendants shall possess the
> gate of their enemies. In your seed all the nations of the earth shall be
> blessed, because you have obeyed My voice." So Abraham returned
> to his young men, and they rose and went together to Beersheba;
> and Abraham dwelt at Beersheba.

First, notice that the Lord provided the sacrifice that Abraham actually
did use. And in return, Abraham called this place "The-Lord-Will-Provide."

He recognized not only that the Lord would save Isaac, but also that He is the provider of all things, from his miraculously conceived child to the very sacrifice that the Lord required.

Then the Lord tells Abraham that He accepts Abraham's complete surrender to His will and will bless this trust in Him by giving Abraham with one of the most valuable things at the time: to be the father of a great nation, whose seed will bless "all the nations of the earth." That fruit of seed, of course, is Jesus.

With great surrender and great obedience, Abraham trusted the Lord in all things, including his child.

There lies my question to you: Have you surrendered your child to the Lord, completely and fully? Are you relying on interventions or your own strength to walk through the difficulties and challenges presented on a daily basis?

Or are you fully and completely handing all things over to Jesus, secure in the knowledge that He can do anything for your or your child, as long as it's in His will? This may mean healing, or it may mean you need to accept things as they are.

Discerning the Lord's Will

It's easy to look at Genesis 22 and say that Abraham had an advantage. After all, the Lord spoke directly to him and there was no mistaking God's will.

But for you and me, it's not always so easy. The truth is we may envy Abraham in this way. Why can't—or won't—God speak clearly and directly to us? Why can't He use words, just as He did with Abraham?

The problem is not the Lord. He speaks to us all the time.

The problem is that we're not listening.

I know that sounds pretty harsh. But I have learned it from my own experience.

How can you discern the Lord's will, regarding your child, or anything in your life, for that matter? You can do this by surrendering all to Him and then clearing the path to allow Him to speak into your life.

The steps are simple but life is demanding and the enemy is constantly prowling. You may have to work at being consistent enough to make sure you are doing these things daily:

Pray Without Ceasing

I know you are thinking, like I once did, "But I can't pray all the time!" And you're partially right. There are times you may need to laser focus on something you are doing. But let's also remember that prayer is not always formal. Prayer is also just talking with God. When we read the Old Testament and see Abraham or Moses talking with God, sometimes it's almost casual. God does not expect us to be 24/7 on our knees in a formal prayer. Yes, we should do that too at times, but we must remember that Jesus is our friend! We can talk to Him any time about our joys, our struggles, our frustrations, and the little things—both good and bad—throughout our day. The more we do this, the more we will see and hear what He has for us.

Quiet Prayer Time

Every day, I make sure that I have quiet time with the Lord. I try to get to bed thirty to sixty minutes before I turn out the light to do my own nighttime routine, including dedicated prayer and scripture time. I use this formula when I pray at night: First, I pray through three Psalms. Then, I pray the ACTS formula that I discussed in Chapter 3.

When thanking Him, I list as many things as I can think of – do not skip this part, even if the only think you can thank Him for is making it through the day. You'll start to see how many "little" things He provides to get you through the day or to bless you as His child.

And finally, remember that while you'll primarily find it easy to pray for your family and your needs, you can pray for all the things that impact our children. This includes laws, school officials, teachers, people who provide services, etc. You can pray for other families as well.

Ask the Lord What You Need to Ask

I know we covered this above, but it's important to be open and honest with Jesus. Remember that He already knows everything, however, He wants you to tell Him those things. This means even if you are angry or disappointed in Him. Just talk to Him! What Jesus wants with you is a relationship. This in no way undermines His Sovereignty as King of the universe. Remember that He is a kind and loving King who wants His followers to come to Him "as little children." So share your heart with God. You are His child, now become His friend and confidante.

Daily Scripture Reading

To truly be His friend, you need to understand Him. And understanding Him can only come from reading His Word regularly. It's important to read something every day, even just a small scripture. Psalms or Proverbs are great for short bites that you can easily consume, so are many of the letters and epistles from the New Testament.But it's also wise to listen to sermons regularly and try to attend a Bible study so you can dig deep into the Word. If you cannot attend a study or go to church in person, sermons are available online from many Bible-believing churches. In fact, most churches nowadays post their sermons to Facebook, YouTube, or other social media.

And you can certainly study the Word with a good devotional or book-based Bible study.

Another resource I love is GotQuestions.org, which answers just about any question on the faith that you can think of.

Doing What He Tells You

Over time – even sometimes rather quickly – the Lord will begin to speak to you and tell you what you need to do. He will use the scriptures to reach out. Sometimes you'll see a verse you've heard dozens of times in a new way. Other times something will jump out at you as the exact answer to a question burning in your heart.

Being able to hear what God wants to say to you takes time and practice. You may think it will be challenging to do these things, but the

Holy Spirit will help you and bless you when you. Then you can walk confidently in the knowledge that you are doing exactly what you should be for your child.

Next, let's go a little deeper into sacrifice and how it brings blessings.

Chapter 24

Naomi and Ruth: Sacrifice Brings Blessings

Then you will experience God's peace, which exceeds anything we can understand. His peace will guard your hearts and minds as you live in Christ Jesus. — Philippians 4:7, NLT

Jesus promised us peace. Now to you this might sound strange, but I have personally experienced that there is only one true road to obtaining His supernatural peace: surrender. It sounds crazy but I have another story to share that will illustrate this point.

More on Surrender: Acceptance with Joy

The words "Acceptance With Joy" are not mine but come from author Hannah Hurnard's book "Hinds' Feet on High Places." The title is drawn from Habakkuk 3:19a (KJV):

> The Lord God is my strength, and he will make my feet like hinds' feet, and he will make me to walk upon mine high places.

Hinds' feet is a reference to deer or mountain goats' feet, that can climb high hills without falling. This verse is also a song, one of joy that states that the Lord will allow you to walk on "high places." What it means is that He will empower you to walk as Christ did even on the difficult and treacherous paths of life.

Hurnard's book is an allegory that tells of a young woman name Much-Afraid and her journey to becoming Joy-With-Acceptance. At the end, she arrives at the High Places, after many trials and temptations, and after making the ultimate surrender. It's well worth the read.

However, even if allegory does not appeal to you, don't worry. The Bible covers what you need in the story of Ruth. This short book has many lessons, but it's near and dear to the heart of many Christian women.

A Jewish woman, Naomi, and her husband leave Israel due a famine and end up in the foreign country of Moab. While there, they have two sons who marry local women Ruth and Orpah.

Shortly after, both Naomi's husband and both her sons die, leaving her and her daughters-in-law destitute. At this period of time in the region, women were completely dependent on men for their provision. If you had no husband, father, or adult son, you were destined for poverty or you had to turn to desperate means, such as prostitution. With no heirs and no caretakers, Naomi decides to return to Israel to take her chances back in her old home. All three women embark on the journey.

Before they arrive, Naomi, who is wracked with grief and what sounds like a sense of hopelessness, begs the younger women to return to their homeland. Orpah does, however, Ruth has a different approach in the first chapter, versus 16-18 (ESV):

> But Ruth said, "Do not urge me to leave you or to return from following you. For where you go I will go, and where you lodge I will lodge. Your people shall be my people, and your God my God. Where you die I will die, and there will I be buried. May the Lord do so to me and more also if anything but death parts me from you." And when Naomi saw that she was determined to go with her, she said no more.

While it would have been easy for Ruth to abandon Naomi, she stayed with her despite her pleadings. Not only did Ruth leave her country and the likelihood of a future marriage, but she also abandoned her country's ways. Moab was a pagan country where they did not worship the God of Israel but their own gods.

To me, this shows that the Lord was already working in Ruth's heart. Whatever her late husband and mother-in-law had taught her about their Jewish faith had seeped down into her soul, turning her from the false religion of her homeland towards the true God.

In this commitment, Ruth gave up everything she knew to be with her mother-in-law and embraced her adopted faith. While you might think Ruth could simply make a fresh start in Israel, that wasn't likely. God forbade Israelite men to marry foreign women. Husbands were often led astray into false religions. When Jewish men married pagan women, they often turned away from Judaism to worship foreign gods throughout the Old Testament.

Even though Ruth was already committed to the Lord, she had to think that she would have no hope of finding a new husband in this new land. Still, she surrendered everything she had to God: her home, her family, and her future.

If you've read Ruth, you know the end of the story. She marries Boaz, who is the grandfather of the great King David, and an ancestor of Jesus. She is richly rewarded for her dedication to both Naomi and the God of Israel. But remember, she had no way of knowing that when she made her covenant to study with Naomi. For all she knew, she'd live out her days alone and in poverty in a foreign land.

But Ruth took the risk. She surrendered absolutely everything to God. Maybe the Lord had spoken to her heart. Maybe there was nothing in Moab for her. Maybe her faith was so strong that she considered it better to be with Naomi in a strange place following the Lord she had accepted than return to her pagan homeland.

We will never know the answer until we get to heaven, but Ruth teaches us many lessons.

What Does Surrender Look Like for Us Parents?

At this point, you may be wondering what surrender looks like for a mom raising a child on the spectrum. For Ruth, surrender required moving away from everything she knew and trusting God to provide. It was a journey that led her to be a poor outcast in a foreign land with no or few visible prospects for the rest of her life. While Ruth was not alone, she didn't have anyone her age or any way to support her family.

Ruth and Naomi were penniless. In order to eat, Ruth was forced to go out into the fields and glean. Gleaning was a practice that poor people used at the time to feed themselves. It simply meant picking up any grain left on the floor after the workers harvested the field.

However, Naomi's late husband had a relative - Boaz – who was kind enough to intentionally allow Ruth to glean from his fields. He makes sure that there is enough left to feed her and Naomi. He even tells her not to glean at any other field. He will provide water for her and make sure that she is protected from any unwanted actions from the harvesters, who were all men.

Ruth falls on her face to thank him and he tells her it's because she cared so well for Naomi. God moved Boaz's heart to notice that she gave up everything to care for her mother-in-law.

Dear friend, God sees you. He sees how much you have given up for your child. He sees your pain and challenges as you wander through the land parenting a child on the spectrum, just as Boaz saw how much Ruth gave up for Naomi.

To continue with the story, Boaz invited Ruth to eat with him at mealtime. So despite having nothing, the Lord provided well for both women, and not just food. Boaz gave Ruth the valuable gift of protection in a day and age when women were extremely vulnerable on their own.

As the story proceeds, Boaz went through all the proper channels and eventually married Ruth. They had a child who became the grandfather of the great King David. Not only that, but Ruth is one of the very few women mentioned in the genealogy of Jesus. These too are rewards for this woman's trust, faith, and devotion to the Lord.

Boaz is Ruth's kinsmen-redeemer. But since we know that every book of the Bible is really just an illustration of Jesus's love, we can interpret this book to mean that it's Jesus who is our kinsman-redeemer.

I want you to stop thinking of either yourself or your spouse as the main provider for your family. Instead, think of Jesus as your family's provider. This is a radical change of thought, but once I did it, I saw God's hand providing work, providing money for bills, providing food on our table, providing for my family, and my business, reducing debt, and showing up for every other need too.

What do you need to surrender to the Lord? There are a few clear things that you can lay down at the feet of Jesus, right now:

1. Provision

The Lord very specifically provides for the needs of His children. In Matthew 6:25-34 (NKJV). Jesus Himself tells us:

> "Therefore I say to you, do not worry about your life, what you will eat or what you will drink; nor about your body, what you will put on. Is not life more than food and the body more than clothing? Look at the birds of the air, for they neither sow nor reap nor gather into barns; yet your heavenly Father feeds them. Are you not of more value than they? Which of you by worrying can add one cubit to his stature?
>
> "So why do you worry about clothing? Consider the lilies of the field, how they grow: they neither toil nor spin; and yet I say to you that even Solomon in all his glory was not arrayed like one of these. Now if God so clothes the grass of the field, which today is, and tomorrow is thrown into the oven, will He not much more clothe you, O you of little faith?
>
> "Therefore do not worry, saying, 'What shall we eat?' or 'What shall we drink?' or 'What shall we wear?' For after all these things the Gentiles seek. For your heavenly Father knows that you need all these things. But seek first the kingdom of God and His righteousness, and all these things shall be added to you. Therefore do not worry about tomorrow, for tomorrow will worry about its own things. Sufficient for the day is its own trouble.

This is not advice for everyone in your family to get up and quit their jobs. It is, however, a call to lean heavily on the Lord when you can't see a way to pay your bills or put food on the table. If you are making choices based on God's will and leading, He will provide, often in a way that brings Him all the glory.

After all, if you can't see the solution and pray earnestly, and then one appears, that is a powerful testimony to the Lord's abundance and grace in your life.

If you have made mistakes, though, that are costing you financially, such as investments or poor choices that have put you in the hole, you may think the Lord will not bail you out.

I have seen firsthand that I can confess my financial misdeeds as sin, repent of them, and beg Him for a way out. One year, my husband and I put a down payment on building a home that we were not meant to have. As our payments piled up, my husband's job was in jeopardy. And then, the economy took a turn for the worse, increasing the amount we'd have to borrow and pay in order to buy a home. That increased our mortgage by a significant amount. In addition, other money we were relying on reduced and my husband's workload dried up.

He was worried but I begged the Lord to save us. And He handled the situation by getting us legally out of the contract and returning every penny back to us.

This is just one example of how He has provided for us, despite our own blunders. Don't limit the Lord. You can trust Him to fix the things you cannot, even your own mistakes.

That said, I've lost count of how many times my husband, our family's main provider, landed a contract right when our cushion of savings was about to run out. Sure, we'd love to be more secure but I have learned that I can trust God to always provide for a roof over our heads, food on the table, utilities, and health needs, no matter what.

2. *Safety*

The Lord wants us to be safe so that we can do the things He has planned for us. Now, keep in mind that God could send you on not-so-safe missions. And He will. If we honestly look at the earthly culture around us, we see that biblical Christianity is frowned upon. We live in a day and age when simply quoting the Bible can get you in trouble and openly living by its precepts can put your livelihood at risk. That is scary.

But if we remember what Jesus has done for us and pray for the Holy Spirit to guide us, He will strengthen us with the courage and the means to do what we must. Look at Abraham. It took courage to walk up that hill to offer his child to the Lord. The Bible is filled with stories of people who did the right thing in the face of odds set against them.

Safety, then, does not mean standing back and letting others fight for their faith. Sometimes you have to take up arms to fight for your family. One example is Deborah and Jael, two women you'll find in the book of Judges. Chapter 4 tells of what they did and Chapter 5 is Deborah's song praising the Lord for victory.

The book of Judges is a challenging book. At the time, judges who were ruling Israel were supposed to follow God's word because in reality, the Lord was ruling Israel during these centuries. However, as a nation, the Israelites were constantly turning away from the Lord. By walking away from the Lord's protection, they would get into trouble with surrounding enemy nations who would attack or wage war on them. They would beg God to save them, then they'd repent and then the whole cycle would start again.

Many chapters begin as Chapter 4 does: "Again the Israelites did evil in the eyes of the Lord..." Whenever this happens, the Lord punishes the Israelites, normally by having their enemies move against them. This time, the Lord sells them into the hands of the Canaanite king Jabin, who oppressed them for twenty years.

Deborah is a female prophet and the only named woman leader – or judge – of the Israelites in the whole Bible. In verse 6, the Lord tells Deborah to call a man named Barak to lead the army. However, Barak told he will only go if she goes. She agrees but informs him that because of this decision, the Lord will hand the victory over the army's commander, Sisera, to a woman.

Deborah knew that leading an army was supposed to be a man's job. She went because Barak did not want to do what the Lord commanded but I have no doubt the Lord prompted her to stand up.

While Barak does defeat the army in the field, Sisera escapes. He makes it to the home of Heber's wife, Jael, who gives him milk and lets him fall asleep – and then kills him with a spike through his head.

Before you go shouting about how great these women were, remember that it was God who brought the enemy to Jael and it was God who made Sisera think that he was safe in Jael's home. It was God who guided Jael to eliminate this evil enemy of the people to fulfill Deborah's prophecy of giving this victory to a woman.

With God's help, you can protect your family by following His leading in all you do, even if you can't get your husband completely on board. Don't go against your spouse's wishes but do follow the Lord's guidance and direction.

3. *Healing*

What happens, though, if one day you see that all the gains your child has made suddenly vanishes? As moms, we tend to blame ourselves. After all, we planned so carefully. We worked, we went to doctors, practitioners, other support staff, we tried diets and protocols and therapies and things were great.

Then you wake up one day and your child has regressed. Maybe she refuses to the use toilet that she mastered years ago, and you must return to diapers. Maybe his meltdowns have returned, stronger than ever. Or aggression and self-injury are on the rise again, and stimming seems constant. Perhaps communication is once again a struggle and academic gains seemed to have disappeared. Maybe you're seeing new and disturbing behavioral or social challenges.

This can happen at the onset of puberty, but it can be triggered by other changes too, or even small things we are not aware of. Our kids have very delicate systems, and it feels like the sword of regression is always hanging over their heads.

Sometimes, it feels like it's our fault. We think, *I didn't try hard enough. I left the protocol too soon. I should have kept that diet for life. I didn't need to do that transition.* This is the time we need to pause. Are you really at fault, or is it simply that your child's body has changed, and you are in a new phase? Maybe they have been exposed to something that wasn't there before, either an environmental toxin, like mold, or a subtler one, like new and complex stressors. Because their biochemistry is so delicate, these changes can come and go, but you might blame yourself for not doing more.

Our kids' delicate systems, though, can only take so much. Everyone needs a break and this progression is really natural. If your child develops a new problem that you aren't aware of, or he or she is exposed to something triggering, these reactions can happen. Not only that, but I have seen even the most astute, diligent, proactive parents discover setbacks in their autistic children at times.

In fact, you may not be able to determine, prevent, or pre-plan everything.

That's why we are going to look at the famous scripture involving Martha and Mary. In this story, Jesus went to visit the two sisters and was hosting a teaching at their home. Martha was getting everything ready for the big event. Luke 10:38-42 (ESV) says:

> Now as they went on their way, Jesus entered a village. And a woman named Martha welcomed Him into her house. And she had a sister called Mary, who sat at the Lord's feet and listened to His teaching. But Martha was distracted with much serving. And she went up to Him and said, "Lord, do you not care that my sister has left me to serve alone? Tell her then to help me." But the Lord answered her, "Martha, Martha, you are anxious and troubled about many things, but one thing is necessary. Mary has chosen the good portion, which will not be taken away from her."

Martha had stopped in the busyness of everything to ogle her sister, sitting at Jesus' feet. And then she had the nerve to complain about the spiritual feeding Mary was receiving, which, according to Jesus, was the "better" part.

I've studied this passage for many years but I'll be honest: I never really thought I was a Martha. I'm not at all a planner, and I'm always getting ready for things at the very last minute. My house is not the cleanest, and I'm ok with that. If you're not, don't come. I'd rather be reading or studying up until the very last minute too.

But as I was working on this chapter, it occurred to me that I've been Martha with my attempts to help my child. I look over at other mothers and see their complete and utter devotion to the Lord in the face of the challenges their child has brought them. Autism is merely part of their life, and they do their best, but wait patiently on the Lord.

They find the blessing in the struggle.

When it comes to healing my child, the hardest thing for me is to sit still and let God do what He will. I was doing everything possible the year my child turned twelve. I had this sort of "ticking clock" over my head.

That year was brutal because she went through puberty and with it, lost gains that we'd accomplished over the years. Watching the regression was extremely difficult.

At the beginning of that year, we were seeing a homeopath and God specifically told me to stop going. It was difficult but I did it, and immediately I brought her to a biomed doctor.

We were going along with very small gains—really, barely any—and I felt this tug. I kept getting the message that God wanted to do what He wanted to do. I took that to mean we needed to stop seeing the biomed doctor too.

GULP. We were…going to do nothing? *Nothing*? But, but, but…

I can hear Martha in my head: "Lord, don't you care that I have to do all this work by myself? Aren't You going to help me?"

And that was exactly when I realized that help and healing does not come from me or my efforts - not ever. It comes from the Hand of God, for God is our kinsman redeemer, just like Boaz was for Ruth and Naomi. He is the God Who provides.

Just like salvation, I cannot choose to bless my child with healing. I can do the best I can, but whatever I do, it must be in God's will.

And if God's will is for me to stop pursuing solutions, then I have to stop. He won't bless my actions if they stem from disobedience.

I tried one more thing that year, but I had to get it refunded right away as soon as I saw it was off course. I took the rest of that year "off" and prayed. God wanted me at His feet, like Mary.

In fact, just shortly after I stopped all interventions, even food, I found that in addition to my stress levels going down, Zoe did make progress. I call it divine progress! God advanced her in areas that she'd been struggling with for at least a decade.

These may be little moves that won't seem earth shattering to most but to me, it's evidence that God can and will move when the timing is right, especially when I surrender everything. And it's a testament to His power, not mine, because He could do what I never could.

However, we weren't done yet because what He really wanted me to surrender was her future.

4. *Our Kids' Future*

I'm not saying you shouldn't plan for your child's future. You should. I cannot give you any advice on this topic, with the exception of get as educated as possible, save whatever you can, and make the best choices for your family...none of which are likely to be ideal or perfect.

That said, while we do need to take action as early as we can and with the Lord's guidance. Sitting around stating, "I can't die," like so many parents I've heard say, is not the way to approach this. God has some wonderful plans for you and your family. Your child may benefit one day from a program that does not even exist yet. Or you may suddenly feel a call to relocate. I know at least two families that felt that way. I'd love to tell you it was smooth, easy sailing, and the new places had everything those families needed. But as often is the case, that's not always how God works. Maybe you need to be the spark that starts something new. Maybe you need the leading of people in that new area. Maybe something you never considered will benefit your child. The point is, your future – and your child's - is safely in God's hands, even if you can't see it right now. Seek His guidance and follow His lead, and you will be O.K. even when what He requires is hard!

And that is the point of leaning on Jesus in all these issues. In the Bible, the Lord told Paul, "My grace is sufficient for you, for My power is made perfect in weakness." What was Paul's response? "Therefore, I will boast all the more gladly of my weaknesses, so that the power of Christ may rest upon me." (2 Corinthians 12:9, ESV) And he continues:

> "For the sake of Christ, then, I am content with weaknesses, insults, hardships, persecutions, and calamities. For when I am weak, then I am strong." (2 Corinthians 12:10, ESV)

Now of course, we can't always wrap our heads around that. But the more we walk with the Lord, the more we learn to lean on Him. And all those crosses we bear can grow a little smaller. Not every single one and not all the time, but He will show you His love and let You see that His way is not just the best way, it's the only way.

As moms, surrender can be difficult. But God has it all in hand, and He is doing great work. Give your child to Him and He will bless your family.

Final Blessing

May God be gracious to us and bless us
and make his face shine on us —
so that your ways may be known on earth,
your salvation among all nations.
May the peoples praise you, God;
may all the peoples praise you.
May the nations be glad and sing for joy,
for you rule the peoples with equity
and guide the nations of the earth.
-Psalm 67: 1-4, ESV

Dear sister in Christ, I hope that this book has helped you and blessed you. There is hope for our autistic children when we walk with the Lord. Jesus has great plans for you and your child. We need to place our trust in Him for everyday things, just as we have trusted Him with our soul.

I want you to look at your beautiful autistic child and see strength, vibrancy, joy, and heart. I want you to discover that he or she has a place and a God-given purpose in this world. I want you to know that you are the absolutely right parent for this child and by walking with Jesus every day, you can find peace and joy in your heart even on the hard days.

I pray that these words have helped you grow closer to Jesus and that you and your child will grow strong in the Lord.

May the peace of Jesus Christ bless you and your family all the days of your lives.

Acknowledgments

Helping moms who raise children with special needs has been something that God put on my heart many years ago. I am grateful that the Lord brought me salvation and given me purpose in life.

I couldn't have written this without my family. I want to thank Amelia and Zoe for being lights that shine in my life even when they struggle and for giving Mom time and space to write and edit!

Thanks to my husband, Chris, who has always supported me in all my endeavors and been right there applauding my achievements. Thank you for your love!

I want to thank Bright Communications for giving me this opportunity and to Jennifer Bright for always showing up with both wisdom and an encouraging smile. Your positivity has helped me get to the end of all those edits.

Thanks to Pam Bartlett for introducing me to Jennifer and to S.E.V.E.N. Networking for bringing us together.

Thank you to the dozens of moms I know who are raising children with different disabilities. I am always inspired by them and how much they sacrifice so their children can have better lives. This book is dedicated to them.

About the Author

Gina Badalaty is a writer, researcher, educator, and entrepreneur. She was born and raised in Queens, New York. She earned her degree in Interdisciplinary Studies at the New York Institute of Technology.

In 2002, Gina and her husband, Chris, moved to Pennsylvania. Gina started one of the first "mom" blogs. She opened a web design shop and ran that for many years before earning her first professional writing gig at American Greeting Cards Interactive in 2008.

By 2014, she was hired by Mamavation to investigate harmful ingredients in products. She's worked with many clean brands and has written for Project NonGMO, Healthy Moms Magazine, Savvy Women's Alliance, and Healthy Child. She wrote for NatualLivingFamily for two years, and she currently writes for FoodRepublic.com.

Gina lives in Pennsylvania with her husband, her two daughters, and their black lab, Bailey. Her children's disabilities have empowered her to be an advocate for people with Down syndrome and people on the autism spectrum. The family enjoys travel, theme parks, and a good sporting or music event.

www.ingramcontent.com/pod-product-compliance
Lightning Source LLC
Chambersburg PA
CBHW071147120626
46546CB00006B/2157